50 Delicious Freezer Meal Recipes for Home

By: Kelly Johnson

Table of Contents

- Beef and Broccoli Stir-Fry
- Chicken Enchiladas
- Vegetable Lasagna
- Thai Green Curry
- Stuffed Bell Peppers
- Spinach and Feta Stuffed Chicken Breasts
- Beef Stew
- Chicken Pot Pie
- Lentil Soup
- Teriyaki Salmon
- Mexican Casserole
- Sausage and Peppers
- BBQ Pulled Pork
- Butternut Squash Soup
- Eggplant Parmesan
- Shrimp Fried Rice
- Turkey Chili
- Chicken Alfredo Pasta Bake
- Greek Chicken Souvlaki
- Shepherd's Pie
- Ratatouille
- Black Bean and Corn Quesadillas
- Italian Wedding Soup
- Lemon Garlic Shrimp
- Beef and Mushroom Stroganoff
- Sweet and Sour Meatballs
- Chicken Curry
- Cheesy Broccoli Rice Casserole
- Pork Carnitas
- Minestrone Soup
- Spaghetti Bolognese
- Chicken Cacciatore
- Beef Burritos
- Creamy Tomato Tortellini Soup
- Veggie-Packed Bolognese Sauce

- Hawaiian Chicken
- Macaroni and Cheese
- Moroccan Tagine
- Sloppy Joes
- Vegetable Curry
- Chicken Tetrazzini
- Pork Tenderloin with Apple Compote
- Buffalo Chicken Wraps
- Mushroom Risotto
- Cajun Jambalaya
- Swedish Meatballs
- Ratatouille Stuffed Peppers
- Korean Beef Bowls
- Creamy Pesto Chicken Pasta
- Veggie-Packed Quinoa Salad

Beef and Broccoli Stir-Fry

Ingredients:

For the Beef Marinade:

- 1 pound flank steak, thinly sliced against the grain
- 2 tablespoons soy sauce
- 1 tablespoon rice vinegar or white vinegar
- 1 tablespoon cornstarch
- 1 teaspoon sesame oil
- 1 teaspoon grated ginger
- 2 cloves garlic, minced
- 1/2 teaspoon black pepper

For the Stir-Fry Sauce:

- 1/4 cup soy sauce
- 2 tablespoons oyster sauce
- 1 tablespoon hoisin sauce
- 1 tablespoon brown sugar or honey
- 1 tablespoon rice vinegar or white vinegar
- 1 teaspoon sesame oil
- 1 teaspoon cornstarch
- 1/4 cup water or beef broth

Other Ingredients:

- 2 tablespoons vegetable oil, divided
- 4 cups broccoli florets
- 1 onion, thinly sliced
- 2 cloves garlic, minced
- Cooked rice, for serving
- Sesame seeds and sliced green onions, for garnish (optional)

Instructions:

1. Marinate the Beef: In a bowl, combine the thinly sliced flank steak with soy sauce, rice vinegar, cornstarch, sesame oil, grated ginger, minced garlic, and black pepper. Mix well to coat the beef evenly with the marinade. Let it marinate for at least 15-20 minutes, or refrigerate for up to 1 hour for more flavor.

2. Prepare the Stir-Fry Sauce: In another bowl, whisk together soy sauce, oyster sauce, hoisin sauce, brown sugar or honey, rice vinegar, sesame oil, cornstarch, and water or beef broth. Set the sauce aside.
3. Stir-Fry the Beef: Heat 1 tablespoon of vegetable oil in a large skillet or wok over high heat. Once hot, add the marinated beef slices in a single layer. Stir-fry for 1-2 minutes until browned and cooked through. Transfer the cooked beef to a plate and set aside.
4. Cook the Broccoli and Onions: In the same skillet or wok, add the remaining 1 tablespoon of vegetable oil. Add the broccoli florets and thinly sliced onion. Stir-fry for 3-4 minutes until the broccoli is tender-crisp and the onions are softened. Add minced garlic and cook for an additional 30 seconds until fragrant.
5. Combine Everything: Return the cooked beef to the skillet or wok with the broccoli and onions. Pour the prepared stir-fry sauce over the beef and vegetables. Stir well to coat everything evenly with the sauce. Cook for an additional 1-2 minutes until the sauce thickens slightly.
6. Serve: Serve the beef and broccoli stir-fry hot over cooked rice. Garnish with sesame seeds and sliced green onions, if desired.
7. Enjoy! This beef and broccoli stir-fry is delicious and packed with flavor. It's a perfect dish for a quick and satisfying weeknight meal.

Chicken Enchiladas

Ingredients:

For the Enchilada Filling:

- 2 cups cooked shredded chicken (rotisserie chicken works well)
- 1 cup shredded cheese (cheddar, Monterey Jack, or a Mexican blend)
- 1 small onion, finely chopped
- 1 bell pepper, diced (optional)
- 2 cloves garlic, minced
- 1 teaspoon ground cumin
- 1 teaspoon chili powder
- Salt and pepper to taste
- 1 tablespoon chopped fresh cilantro (optional)

For the Enchilada Sauce:

- 2 tablespoons vegetable oil
- 2 tablespoons all-purpose flour
- 2 tablespoons chili powder
- 1 teaspoon ground cumin
- 1/2 teaspoon garlic powder
- 1/4 teaspoon dried oregano

- 2 cups chicken broth
- 1 can (8 ounces) tomato sauce
- Salt to taste

Other Ingredients:

- 10-12 corn tortillas
- Additional shredded cheese for topping
- Chopped fresh cilantro for garnish
- Sour cream and diced avocado for serving (optional)

Instructions:

Prepare the Enchilada Filling:

1. Preheat the oven to 350°F (175°C). Lightly grease a 9x13-inch baking dish.
2. In a large skillet, heat a tablespoon of oil over medium heat. Add the chopped onion and bell pepper (if using) and sauté until softened, about 5 minutes. Add the minced garlic and cook for an additional 1 minute.
3. Add the shredded chicken, ground cumin, chili powder, salt, pepper, and chopped cilantro (if using) to the skillet. Stir well to combine and cook for another 2-3 minutes until heated through. Remove from heat and set aside.

Prepare the Enchilada Sauce:

1. In a saucepan, heat 2 tablespoons of vegetable oil over medium heat. Stir in the all-purpose flour and cook for 1-2 minutes to make a roux.
2. Add the chili powder, ground cumin, garlic powder, and dried oregano to the roux. Cook for another minute, stirring constantly, until fragrant.
3. Gradually whisk in the chicken broth and tomato sauce until smooth. Bring the sauce to a simmer and cook for 5-7 minutes, stirring occasionally, until thickened. Season with salt to taste.

Assemble the Enchiladas:

1. Pour a thin layer of enchilada sauce into the bottom of the prepared baking dish.
2. Warm the corn tortillas in the microwave or on a skillet for a few seconds until pliable.
3. Spoon a portion of the chicken filling onto each tortilla and sprinkle with shredded cheese. Roll up the tortillas tightly and place them seam-side down in the baking dish.
4. Pour the remaining enchilada sauce over the rolled tortillas, spreading it evenly to cover them. Sprinkle with additional shredded cheese on top.
5. Cover the baking dish with aluminum foil and bake in the preheated oven for 20-25 minutes, or until the enchiladas are heated through and the cheese is melted and bubbly.

6. Remove the foil and bake for an additional 5 minutes until the cheese is lightly browned.
7. Garnish with chopped fresh cilantro and serve hot with sour cream and diced avocado, if desired.

Enjoy these delicious chicken enchiladas as a hearty and flavorful meal!

Vegetable Lasagna

Ingredients:

For the Vegetable Filling:

- 2 tablespoons olive oil
- 1 onion, finely chopped
- 2 cloves garlic, minced
- 1 medium zucchini, diced
- 1 medium yellow squash, diced
- 1 red bell pepper, diced
- 1 yellow bell pepper, diced
- 2 cups sliced mushrooms
- 1 teaspoon dried oregano
- 1 teaspoon dried basil
- Salt and pepper to taste
- 1 can (14 ounces) diced tomatoes, drained
- 1 cup marinara sauce

For the Cheese Mixture:

- 15 ounces ricotta cheese
- 1/2 cup grated Parmesan cheese
- 1 egg
- 2 tablespoons chopped fresh parsley
- Salt and pepper to taste

Other Ingredients:

- 9 lasagna noodles, cooked according to package instructions
- 2 cups shredded mozzarella cheese
- Additional grated Parmesan cheese for topping
- Fresh basil leaves for garnish (optional)

Instructions:

1. Prepare the Vegetable Filling:
   - In a large skillet, heat the olive oil over medium heat. Add the chopped onion and minced garlic, and sauté until softened and fragrant, about 2-3 minutes.
   - Add the diced zucchini, yellow squash, red bell pepper, yellow bell pepper, and sliced mushrooms to the skillet. Cook, stirring occasionally, for 5-7 minutes until the vegetables are tender.
   - Season the vegetables with dried oregano, dried basil, salt, and pepper. Stir in the diced tomatoes and marinara sauce. Cook for another 2-3 minutes, then remove from heat. Set aside.
2. Prepare the Cheese Mixture:
   - In a mixing bowl, combine the ricotta cheese, grated Parmesan cheese, egg, chopped fresh parsley, salt, and pepper. Mix until well combined. Set aside.
3. Assemble the Lasagna:
   - Preheat the oven to 375°F (190°C). Grease a 9x13-inch baking dish.
   - Spread a thin layer of the vegetable filling on the bottom of the baking dish.
   - Place three cooked lasagna noodles on top of the vegetable filling.
   - Spread half of the cheese mixture over the noodles, followed by half of the remaining vegetable filling. Sprinkle with a layer of shredded mozzarella cheese.
   - Repeat the layers: three lasagna noodles, remaining cheese mixture, remaining vegetable filling, and another layer of shredded mozzarella cheese.
   - Top with the remaining three lasagna noodles. Spread any remaining vegetable filling over the top layer of noodles.
   - Sprinkle with additional shredded mozzarella cheese and grated Parmesan cheese.
4. Bake the Lasagna:
   - Cover the baking dish with aluminum foil and bake in the preheated oven for 30 minutes.
   - Remove the foil and bake for an additional 10-15 minutes, or until the cheese is melted and bubbly, and the lasagna is heated through.
5. Serve:
   - Remove the vegetable lasagna from the oven and let it cool for a few minutes before slicing.
   - Garnish with fresh basil leaves, if desired.
   - Serve hot and enjoy this delicious and hearty vegetable lasagna!

This vegetable lasagna is packed with flavor and wholesome ingredients, making it a satisfying meal for any occasion. Feel free to customize it by adding your favorite vegetables or using different types of cheese.

Thai Green Curry

Ingredients:

For the Green Curry Paste:

- 2 shallots, chopped
- 4 cloves garlic, chopped
- 2 stalks lemongrass, chopped (tough outer layer removed)
- 1-inch piece of galangal or ginger, chopped
- 2 green Thai chilies, chopped (adjust to taste)
- 1 bunch fresh cilantro, stems and leaves separated
- 1 teaspoon ground coriander
- 1 teaspoon ground cumin
- 1/2 teaspoon ground white pepper
- 1/2 teaspoon shrimp paste (optional, omit for vegetarian/vegan)
- Zest of 1 lime
- 2 tablespoons vegetable oil

For the Curry:

- 1 tablespoon vegetable oil
- 1 pound chicken, beef, shrimp, or tofu, cut into bite-sized pieces
- 1 can (14 ounces) coconut milk
- 1 cup chicken or vegetable broth
- 2 tablespoons fish sauce or soy sauce (for vegetarian/vegan)
- 2 teaspoons palm sugar or brown sugar
- 1 cup assorted vegetables (such as bell peppers, bamboo shoots, eggplant, green beans)
- Fresh basil leaves or Thai basil leaves, for garnish
- Cooked rice, for serving

Instructions:

Make the Green Curry Paste:

1. In a food processor or blender, combine the chopped shallots, garlic, lemongrass, galangal or ginger, green Thai chilies, cilantro stems, ground coriander, ground cumin, ground white pepper, shrimp paste (if using), and lime zest.
2. Blend the ingredients until smooth, adding the vegetable oil gradually to help emulsify the mixture. You may need to scrape down the sides of the processor or blender occasionally to ensure everything is well combined.

Prepare the Curry:

1. Heat 1 tablespoon of vegetable oil in a large skillet or wok over medium-high heat. Add the green curry paste and cook for 1-2 minutes, stirring constantly, until fragrant.
2. Add the chicken, beef, shrimp, or tofu to the skillet and cook until browned and cooked through.
3. Pour in the coconut milk and chicken or vegetable broth. Stir in the fish sauce or soy sauce and palm sugar or brown sugar. Bring the mixture to a simmer.
4. Add the assorted vegetables to the skillet and simmer for 5-7 minutes, or until the vegetables are tender and cooked through.
5. Taste the curry and adjust the seasoning, adding more fish sauce or soy sauce, sugar, or green curry paste as needed to achieve the desired flavor.
6. Serve the green curry hot over cooked rice. Garnish with fresh basil leaves or Thai basil leaves.
7. Enjoy your delicious Thai green curry!

Feel free to customize this recipe by using your favorite protein and vegetables. You can also adjust the spiciness of the curry by adding more or fewer green Thai chilies.

Stuffed Bell Peppers

Ingredients:

- 4 large bell peppers (any color)
- 1 tablespoon olive oil
- 1 onion, diced
- 2 cloves garlic, minced
- 1 pound ground beef, turkey, or chicken
- 1 cup cooked rice (white or brown)
- 1 can (14 ounces) diced tomatoes, drained

- 1 cup shredded cheese (cheddar, mozzarella, or a blend)
- 1 teaspoon dried oregano
- 1 teaspoon dried basil
- Salt and pepper to taste
- Fresh parsley or cilantro for garnish (optional)

Instructions:

1. Prepare the Bell Peppers:
    - Preheat your oven to 375°F (190°C).
    - Cut the tops off the bell peppers and remove the seeds and membranes from inside. Trim the bottoms slightly if needed so that they stand upright in a baking dish.
    - Bring a large pot of salted water to a boil. Add the bell peppers and blanch them for 3-4 minutes to slightly soften. Remove them from the water and set aside to cool.
2. Prepare the Filling:
    - In a large skillet, heat the olive oil over medium heat. Add the diced onion and minced garlic, and cook until softened and fragrant, about 3-4 minutes.
    - Add the ground meat to the skillet and cook until browned, breaking it up with a spoon as it cooks.
    - Once the meat is cooked through, drain any excess fat from the skillet.
    - Stir in the cooked rice, diced tomatoes, shredded cheese, dried oregano, dried basil, salt, and pepper. Mix well to combine.
3. Stuff the Bell Peppers:
    - Spoon the filling mixture into the blanched bell peppers, pressing down gently to pack the filling.
    - Place the stuffed bell peppers upright in a baking dish. If necessary, use foil or crumpled parchment paper to help them stand upright.
4. Bake:
    - Cover the baking dish with foil and bake in the preheated oven for 25-30 minutes.
    - Remove the foil and bake for an additional 10-15 minutes, or until the peppers are tender and the filling is heated through.
5. Serve:
    - Remove the stuffed bell peppers from the oven and let them cool for a few minutes before serving.

- Garnish with fresh parsley or cilantro if desired.
- Serve hot and enjoy!

These stuffed bell peppers make for a hearty and satisfying meal. You can also customize the filling by adding additional vegetables, beans, or spices to suit your taste preferences.

Spinach and Feta Stuffed Chicken Breasts

Ingredients:

- 4 boneless, skinless chicken breasts
- Salt and pepper to taste
- 2 cups fresh spinach leaves
- 1/2 cup crumbled feta cheese
- 2 tablespoons olive oil
- 2 cloves garlic, minced
- 1 teaspoon dried oregano
- 1 teaspoon dried basil
- 1/2 teaspoon paprika
- Toothpicks or kitchen twine (optional)

Instructions:

1. Preheat the Oven: Preheat your oven to 375°F (190°C). Grease a baking dish large enough to fit the chicken breasts in a single layer.
2. Prepare the Chicken Breasts:
    - Place each chicken breast between two sheets of plastic wrap or wax paper.
    - Use a meat mallet or rolling pin to gently pound the chicken breasts to an even thickness of about 1/2 inch. This will make it easier to stuff and roll them.
3. Season the Chicken:
    - Season both sides of each chicken breast with salt and pepper to taste.
4. Prepare the Filling:
    - In a skillet, heat 1 tablespoon of olive oil over medium heat. Add the minced garlic and cook for 1-2 minutes until fragrant.
    - Add the fresh spinach leaves to the skillet and cook, stirring, until wilted, about 2-3 minutes.
    - Remove the skillet from the heat and let the spinach cool slightly. Once cooled, stir in the crumbled feta cheese.
5. Stuff the Chicken Breasts:

- Spoon the spinach and feta mixture onto one half of each chicken breast, dividing it evenly among them.
- Carefully fold the other half of each chicken breast over the filling to enclose it. If needed, use toothpicks or kitchen twine to secure the edges and keep the filling from falling out.

6. Season the Chicken:
    - In a small bowl, mix together the dried oregano, dried basil, and paprika.
    - Brush the stuffed chicken breasts with the remaining tablespoon of olive oil, then sprinkle the herb and spice mixture evenly over the tops.
7. Bake the Chicken:
    - Place the stuffed chicken breasts in the prepared baking dish.
    - Bake in the preheated oven for 25-30 minutes, or until the chicken is cooked through and reaches an internal temperature of 165°F (74°C).
8. Serve:
    - Remove the stuffed chicken breasts from the oven and let them rest for a few minutes before serving.
    - Serve hot, garnished with additional fresh herbs if desired.

Enjoy these delicious spinach and feta stuffed chicken breasts as a flavorful and satisfying main course!

Beef Stew

Ingredients:

- 2 pounds stewing beef, cut into 1-inch cubes
- Salt and pepper to taste
- 1/4 cup all-purpose flour
- 2 tablespoons vegetable oil or olive oil
- 1 onion, chopped
- 3 cloves garlic, minced
- 4 cups beef broth
- 1 cup red wine (optional)
- 2 bay leaves
- 1 teaspoon dried thyme
- 1 teaspoon dried rosemary
- 4 carrots, peeled and cut into chunks
- 3 stalks celery, chopped
- 2 potatoes, peeled and cut into chunks
- 1 cup frozen peas (optional)
- Chopped fresh parsley for garnish (optional)

Instructions:

1. **Prepare the Beef:**
    - Season the beef cubes with salt and pepper, then coat them in the all-purpose flour, shaking off any excess.
2. **Brown the Beef:**
    - Heat the vegetable oil or olive oil in a large pot or Dutch oven over medium-high heat.
    - Add the beef cubes in batches and cook until browned on all sides, about 5-7 minutes per batch. Transfer the browned beef to a plate and set aside.
3. **Saute the Aromatics:**
    - In the same pot, add the chopped onion and cook until softened, about 3-4 minutes.
    - Add the minced garlic and cook for an additional 1 minute until fragrant.
4. **Deglaze the Pot:**
    - Pour in the beef broth and red wine (if using), scraping up any browned bits from the bottom of the pot.
5. **Simmer the Stew:**
    - Return the browned beef cubes to the pot.
    - Add the bay leaves, dried thyme, and dried rosemary.
    - Bring the mixture to a simmer, then reduce the heat to low. Cover the pot and let the stew simmer for 1 to 1 1/2 hours, stirring occasionally, until the beef is tender.
6. **Add the Vegetables:**
    - Add the carrots, celery, and potatoes to the pot.
    - Continue to simmer, covered, for an additional 30-45 minutes, or until the vegetables are tender and the flavors have melded together.
7. **Finish the Stew:**
    - If using, add the frozen peas to the pot during the last 5 minutes of cooking.
    - Taste the stew and adjust the seasoning with salt and pepper if needed.
8. **Serve:**
    - Ladle the beef stew into bowls and garnish with chopped fresh parsley if desired.
    - Serve hot and enjoy this comforting and delicious meal!

Beef stew is even better the next day, so feel free to make it ahead of time and reheat it when you're ready to eat. It also freezes well for longer storage.

Chicken Pot Pie

Ingredients:

For the Pie Crust:

- 2 1/2 cups all-purpose flour
- 1 teaspoon salt
- 1 cup cold unsalted butter, cut into cubes
- 6-8 tablespoons ice water

For the Filling:

- 2 tablespoons unsalted butter
- 1 onion, chopped
- 2 carrots, diced
- 2 stalks celery, diced
- 3 cloves garlic, minced
- 1/3 cup all-purpose flour
- 2 cups chicken broth
- 1 cup milk
- 2 cups cooked chicken, diced or shredded
- 1 cup frozen peas
- Salt and pepper to taste
- 1 teaspoon dried thyme
- 1 teaspoon dried parsley
- 1 egg, beaten (for egg wash)

Instructions:

For the Pie Crust:

1. Prepare the Dough: In a large mixing bowl, whisk together the all-purpose flour and salt. Add the cold cubed butter and use a pastry cutter or your fingers to work the butter into the flour until the mixture resembles coarse crumbs.
2. Add Water: Gradually add the ice water, a tablespoon at a time, mixing with a fork until the dough comes together. Be careful not to overwork the dough. Divide the dough in half, shape each half into a disk, wrap them in plastic wrap, and refrigerate for at least 30 minutes.

For the Filling:

1. Preheat the Oven: Preheat your oven to 400°F (200°C). Grease a 9-inch pie dish.
2. Prepare the Filling: In a large skillet, melt the butter over medium heat. Add the chopped onion, diced carrots, and diced celery. Cook for 5-7 minutes until the vegetables are softened.
3. Add Flavor: Add the minced garlic and cook for an additional minute until fragrant.

4. **Thicken the Sauce:** Sprinkle the flour over the vegetables and stir to coat. Cook for 1-2 minutes, then gradually pour in the chicken broth and milk, stirring constantly to prevent lumps from forming. Cook until the mixture thickens, about 5 minutes.
5. **Add Chicken and Peas:** Stir in the cooked chicken, frozen peas, dried thyme, dried parsley, salt, and pepper. Remove the skillet from heat and set aside.

Assemble the Pie:

1. **Roll Out the Dough:** On a lightly floured surface, roll out one disk of the chilled pie dough into a circle large enough to line the bottom and sides of the pie dish. Carefully transfer the rolled-out dough to the greased pie dish.
2. **Add the Filling:** Spoon the chicken and vegetable filling into the prepared pie crust, spreading it out evenly.
3. **Cover with the Top Crust:** Roll out the second disk of pie dough into a circle large enough to cover the filling. Place the rolled-out dough over the filling and crimp the edges to seal the pie. Use a sharp knife to make a few small slits in the top crust to allow steam to escape.
4. **Brush with Egg Wash:** Brush the top crust with the beaten egg, which will give the pie a golden brown color when baked.
5. **Bake:** Place the assembled pie on a baking sheet (to catch any drips) and bake in the preheated oven for 35-40 minutes, or until the crust is golden brown and the filling is bubbly.
6. **Serve:** Remove the chicken pot pie from the oven and let it cool for a few minutes before slicing. Serve hot and enjoy this comforting and delicious meal!

Chicken pot pie is a versatile dish, so feel free to customize it by adding your favorite herbs or vegetables to the filling. It's the perfect comfort food for a chilly evening!

Lentil Soup

Ingredients:

- 1 cup dried lentils (any variety), rinsed and drained
- 1 tablespoon olive oil
- 1 onion, chopped
- 2 carrots, diced
- 2 stalks celery, diced
- 3 cloves garlic, minced
- 1 teaspoon ground cumin
- 1 teaspoon ground coriander
- 1/2 teaspoon smoked paprika
- 6 cups vegetable or chicken broth

- 1 bay leaf
- Salt and pepper to taste
- 2 cups fresh spinach or kale, chopped
- Juice of 1 lemon
- Chopped fresh parsley for garnish (optional)

Instructions:

1. Prepare the Lentils:
   - Rinse the lentils under cold water and drain them. Set aside.
2. Saute Aromatics:
   - In a large pot or Dutch oven, heat the olive oil over medium heat. Add the chopped onion, diced carrots, and diced celery. Cook, stirring occasionally, until the vegetables are softened, about 5-7 minutes.
   - Add the minced garlic, ground cumin, ground coriander, and smoked paprika. Cook for an additional 1-2 minutes until fragrant.
3. Simmer the Soup:
   - Add the rinsed and drained lentils to the pot.
   - Pour in the vegetable or chicken broth and add the bay leaf.
   - Season with salt and pepper to taste.
   - Bring the soup to a boil, then reduce the heat to low. Cover the pot and let the soup simmer for 20-25 minutes, or until the lentils are tender.
4. Add Greens and Lemon Juice:
   - Stir in the chopped spinach or kale and let it wilt in the hot soup for a few minutes.
   - Remove the pot from the heat and discard the bay leaf.
   - Stir in the lemon juice to brighten the flavors of the soup.
5. Serve:
   - Ladle the lentil soup into bowls.
   - Garnish with chopped fresh parsley, if desired.
   - Serve hot and enjoy this comforting and nutritious meal!

Lentil soup is versatile, so feel free to customize it by adding other vegetables or herbs according to your taste preferences. It's a great way to warm up on a cold day and it's packed with protein and fiber from the lentils and vegetables.

Teriyaki Salmon

Ingredients:

- 4 salmon fillets (about 6 ounces each)
- 1/4 cup soy sauce
- 2 tablespoons honey or maple syrup
- 2 tablespoons rice vinegar
- 2 cloves garlic, minced
- 1 teaspoon grated ginger
- 1 tablespoon cornstarch
- 1 tablespoon water
- Optional garnishes: sliced green onions, sesame seeds

Instructions:

1. Prepare the Teriyaki Sauce:
    - In a small saucepan, combine the soy sauce, honey or maple syrup, rice vinegar, minced garlic, and grated ginger.
    - Bring the mixture to a simmer over medium heat, stirring occasionally. Let it simmer for 1-2 minutes to allow the flavors to meld.
2. Thicken the Sauce:
    - In a small bowl, mix the cornstarch with water to create a slurry.
    - Gradually pour the slurry into the simmering sauce, stirring constantly.
    - Continue to cook for another 1-2 minutes, or until the sauce thickens to your desired consistency. Remove from heat.
3. Marinate the Salmon:
    - Place the salmon fillets in a shallow dish or resealable plastic bag.
    - Pour half of the teriyaki sauce over the salmon, reserving the other half for later.
    - Let the salmon marinate in the sauce for at least 15-30 minutes in the refrigerator, allowing the flavors to penetrate the fish.
4. Cook the Salmon:
    - Preheat your oven to 400°F (200°C).
    - Line a baking sheet with parchment paper or aluminum foil for easy cleanup.
    - Place the marinated salmon fillets on the prepared baking sheet, skin-side down.
    - Bake in the preheated oven for 12-15 minutes, or until the salmon is cooked through and flakes easily with a fork.
5. Glaze the Salmon:

- About halfway through the cooking time, brush the reserved teriyaki sauce over the salmon fillets for added flavor and shine.
- Continue baking until the salmon is done.
6. Serve:
    - Once the salmon is cooked, remove it from the oven and let it rest for a few minutes.
    - Transfer the salmon fillets to serving plates and garnish with sliced green onions and sesame seeds, if desired.
    - Serve hot with rice and steamed vegetables for a complete meal.

Enjoy this delicious and succulent teriyaki salmon as a healthy and satisfying dinner option!

Mexican Casserole

Ingredients:

- 1 pound ground beef
- 1 onion, chopped
- 2 cloves garlic, minced
- 1 bell pepper, chopped (any color)
- 1 can (15 ounces) black beans, drained and rinsed
- 1 can (15 ounces) corn, drained
- 1 can (10 ounces) diced tomatoes with green chilies (such as Rotel)
- 1 packet (1 ounce) taco seasoning
- 1 cup salsa
- 6-8 large flour tortillas
- 2 cups shredded cheese (cheddar, Monterey Jack, or a Mexican blend)
- Optional toppings: sliced green onions, diced tomatoes, chopped cilantro, sour cream, sliced jalapeños

Instructions:

1. Preheat the Oven: Preheat your oven to 375°F (190°C). Grease a 9x13-inch baking dish.
2. Cook the Beef Mixture:
    - In a large skillet, cook the ground beef over medium heat until browned and cooked through, breaking it up with a spoon as it cooks.
    - Add the chopped onion, minced garlic, and chopped bell pepper to the skillet. Cook for an additional 3-5 minutes until the vegetables are softened.

3. Add Beans, Corn, and Tomatoes:
   - Stir in the black beans, corn, diced tomatoes with green chilies, and taco seasoning. Mix well to combine.
   - Let the mixture simmer for 5-7 minutes, stirring occasionally, to allow the flavors to meld together.
4. Assemble the Casserole:
   - Spread a thin layer of salsa on the bottom of the prepared baking dish.
   - Place a layer of flour tortillas on top of the salsa, overlapping them slightly to cover the bottom of the dish.
   - Spoon half of the beef and bean mixture over the tortillas, spreading it out evenly.
   - Sprinkle a layer of shredded cheese over the beef mixture.
   - Repeat the layers: tortillas, beef mixture, cheese, ending with a layer of cheese on top.
5. Bake:
   - Cover the baking dish with aluminum foil and bake in the preheated oven for 25-30 minutes.
   - Remove the foil and bake for an additional 10-15 minutes, or until the cheese is melted and bubbly, and the casserole is heated through.
6. Serve:
   - Remove the Mexican casserole from the oven and let it cool for a few minutes before serving.
   - Garnish with your favorite toppings such as sliced green onions, diced tomatoes, chopped cilantro, sour cream, and sliced jalapeños.
   - Serve hot and enjoy this delicious and satisfying meal!

Mexican casserole is a crowd-pleaser and can be easily customized to suit your taste preferences. Feel free to add other ingredients like olives, green chilies, or diced jalapeños for extra flavor and spice.

Sausage and Peppers

Ingredients:

- 1 pound Italian sausage links (sweet or hot), sliced into 1-inch pieces
- 2 tablespoons olive oil
- 1 onion, thinly sliced
- 2 bell peppers (any color), sliced
- 3 cloves garlic, minced
- 1 can (14.5 ounces) diced tomatoes
- 1 teaspoon dried oregano

- 1 teaspoon dried basil
- Salt and pepper to taste
- Optional: crushed red pepper flakes for extra heat
- Fresh parsley or basil for garnish (optional)
- Crusty bread or cooked pasta for serving

Instructions:

1. Cook the Sausage:
    - Heat the olive oil in a large skillet or Dutch oven over medium heat. Add the sliced sausage pieces and cook until browned on all sides, about 5-7 minutes. Remove the sausage from the skillet and set aside.
2. Saute the Vegetables:
    - In the same skillet, add the sliced onion and bell peppers. Cook, stirring occasionally, until the vegetables are softened and slightly caramelized, about 8-10 minutes.
    - Add the minced garlic to the skillet and cook for an additional 1-2 minutes until fragrant.
3. Combine and Simmer:
    - Return the cooked sausage to the skillet with the sautéed vegetables.
    - Pour in the diced tomatoes with their juices.
    - Stir in the dried oregano and dried basil. Season with salt and pepper to taste.
    - If you like extra heat, you can add some crushed red pepper flakes at this point.
    - Stir everything together and bring the mixture to a simmer.
4. Simmer:
    - Reduce the heat to low, cover the skillet, and let the sausage and peppers simmer for 15-20 minutes to allow the flavors to meld together.
5. Serve:
    - Once the sausage and peppers are cooked and tender, remove the skillet from the heat.
    - Garnish with chopped fresh parsley or basil, if desired.
    - Serve hot, spooned over crusty bread or cooked pasta, or enjoy it on its own.

Sausage and peppers is a versatile dish that can be served as a main course, sandwich filling, or even as a topping for pizza or pasta. It's a comforting and satisfying meal that's perfect for busy weeknights or casual gatherings.

BBQ Pulled Pork

Ingredients:

- 3-4 pounds pork shoulder or pork butt
- Salt and pepper to taste
- 1 tablespoon olive oil
- 1 onion, chopped
- 3 cloves garlic, minced
- 1 cup BBQ sauce (homemade or store-bought)
- 1/2 cup chicken or vegetable broth
- 2 tablespoons brown sugar
- 2 tablespoons apple cider vinegar
- 1 tablespoon Worcestershire sauce
- 1 teaspoon smoked paprika
- 1/2 teaspoon ground cumin
- 1/2 teaspoon chili powder
- Hamburger buns or sandwich rolls, for serving

Instructions:

1. Prepare the Pork:
    - Trim any excess fat from the pork shoulder or pork butt. Season all sides generously with salt and pepper.
2. Sear the Pork:
    - In a large skillet or Dutch oven, heat the olive oil over medium-high heat. Add the seasoned pork and sear on all sides until browned, about 3-4 minutes per side. This step helps to develop flavor.
3. Saute Aromatics:
    - Add the chopped onion to the skillet and cook until softened, about 3-4 minutes. Add the minced garlic and cook for an additional minute until fragrant.
4. Prepare the Sauce:
    - In a bowl, mix together the BBQ sauce, chicken or vegetable broth, brown sugar, apple cider vinegar, Worcestershire sauce, smoked paprika, ground cumin, and chili powder until well combined.
5. Combine and Cook:
    - Place the seared pork back into the skillet or Dutch oven. Pour the BBQ sauce mixture over the pork, ensuring it's well coated.
    - Bring the mixture to a simmer, then reduce the heat to low. Cover and let it cook for 6-8 hours, or until the pork is tender and easily shreds with a fork. Alternatively, you can transfer everything to a slow cooker and cook on low for 8 hours or high for 4-5 hours.
6. Shred the Pork:
    - Once the pork is cooked, use two forks to shred it directly in the skillet or Dutch oven. Mix the shredded pork with the sauce to ensure it's evenly coated.

7. Serve:
    - Serve the BBQ pulled pork hot on hamburger buns or sandwich rolls. You can also serve it alongside coleslaw, pickles, or your favorite BBQ sides.

This BBQ pulled pork is sure to be a crowd-pleaser at any gathering. Enjoy the delicious flavors and tender texture of this classic dish!

Butternut Squash Soup

Ingredients:

- 1 medium-sized butternut squash (about 2 pounds), peeled, seeded, and chopped
- 1 tablespoon olive oil
- 1 onion, chopped
- 2 carrots, chopped
- 2 stalks celery, chopped
- 3 cloves garlic, minced
- 4 cups vegetable or chicken broth
- 1 teaspoon dried thyme
- 1/2 teaspoon ground cinnamon
- Salt and pepper to taste
- 1/2 cup heavy cream or coconut cream (for a dairy-free option)
- Optional garnishes: chopped fresh parsley, a drizzle of cream, toasted pumpkin seeds, croutons

Instructions:

1. Roast the Butternut Squash:
    - Preheat your oven to 400°F (200°C).
    - Place the chopped butternut squash on a baking sheet lined with parchment paper.
    - Drizzle with olive oil and season with salt and pepper.
    - Roast in the preheated oven for 25-30 minutes, or until the squash is tender and lightly caramelized. Remove from the oven and set aside.
2. Saute the Vegetables:
    - In a large pot or Dutch oven, heat the olive oil over medium heat.
    - Add the chopped onion, carrots, and celery. Cook, stirring occasionally, until the vegetables are softened, about 5-7 minutes.
    - Add the minced garlic and cook for an additional 1-2 minutes until fragrant.
3. Simmer the Soup:

- Add the roasted butternut squash to the pot.
- Pour in the vegetable or chicken broth to cover the vegetables. Add more broth if needed.
- Stir in the dried thyme and ground cinnamon. Season with salt and pepper to taste.
- Bring the mixture to a simmer, then reduce the heat to low. Cover the pot and let the soup simmer for 15-20 minutes to allow the flavors to meld together.

4. Blend the Soup:
   - Once the soup is cooked and the vegetables are tender, remove the pot from the heat.
   - Use an immersion blender to blend the soup until smooth and creamy. Alternatively, you can carefully transfer the soup in batches to a blender and blend until smooth. Be cautious as the soup will be hot.

5. Add Cream:
   - Stir in the heavy cream or coconut cream, if using. Adjust the consistency of the soup by adding more broth if desired.

6. Serve:
   - Ladle the butternut squash soup into bowls.
   - Garnish with chopped fresh parsley, a drizzle of cream, toasted pumpkin seeds, or croutons if desired.
   - Serve hot and enjoy this creamy and delicious soup!

Butternut squash soup is perfect for a cozy meal and can be easily customized with your favorite spices and garnishes. Enjoy its comforting flavors!

Eggplant Parmesan

Ingredients:

- 2 large eggplants, sliced into 1/2-inch rounds
- Salt
- 2 cups breadcrumbs (plain or Italian-seasoned)
- 1 cup all-purpose flour
- 4 large eggs, beaten
- 1/4 cup grated Parmesan cheese
- 2 cups marinara sauce (homemade or store-bought)
- 2 cups shredded mozzarella cheese
- 1/2 cup grated Parmesan cheese
- Fresh basil leaves, for garnish (optional)

Instructions:

1. **Preheat the Oven:** Preheat your oven to 375°F (190°C). Grease a baking sheet with olive oil or cooking spray.
2. **Prepare the Eggplant:**
   - Place the eggplant slices on a wire rack set over a baking sheet. Sprinkle both sides of the eggplant slices generously with salt. Let them sit for about 30 minutes to release excess moisture.
   - After 30 minutes, pat the eggplant slices dry with paper towels to remove the excess moisture.
3. **Bread the Eggplant:**
   - Set up a breading station with three shallow dishes: one with all-purpose flour, one with beaten eggs, and one with breadcrumbs mixed with 1/4 cup grated Parmesan cheese.
   - Dredge each eggplant slice in the flour, shaking off any excess. Dip it into the beaten eggs, then coat it in the breadcrumb mixture, pressing gently to adhere. Repeat with all eggplant slices.
4. **Fry the Eggplant:**
   - Heat about 1/4 inch of olive oil in a large skillet over medium heat. Once the oil is hot, add the breaded eggplant slices in a single layer, working in batches if necessary.
   - Cook the eggplant slices until golden brown and crispy on both sides, about 3-4 minutes per side. Transfer the fried eggplant slices to a plate lined with paper towels to drain excess oil.
5. **Assemble the Eggplant Parmesan:**
   - Spread a thin layer of marinara sauce on the bottom of a 9x13-inch baking dish.
   - Arrange a layer of fried eggplant slices on top of the sauce, overlapping slightly.
   - Spoon marinara sauce over the eggplant slices, then sprinkle shredded mozzarella cheese and grated Parmesan cheese over the sauce.
   - Repeat the layers until all the eggplant slices are used, finishing with a layer of marinara sauce and cheese on top.
6. **Bake:**
   - Cover the baking dish with aluminum foil and bake in the preheated oven for 25-30 minutes.
   - Remove the foil and bake for an additional 10-15 minutes, or until the cheese is melted and bubbly and the eggplant is tender.
7. **Serve:**
   - Remove the eggplant Parmesan from the oven and let it cool for a few minutes before serving.
   - Garnish with fresh basil leaves, if desired.
   - Serve hot and enjoy this classic Italian dish!

Eggplant Parmesan is delicious served with pasta or crusty bread. It's a crowd-pleasing dish that's perfect for family dinners or special occasions.

Shrimp Fried Rice

Ingredients:

- 2 cups cooked rice (preferably day-old rice, chilled)
- 1 pound large shrimp, peeled and deveined
- 2 tablespoons soy sauce
- 1 tablespoon oyster sauce (optional)
- 1 tablespoon sesame oil
- 2 tablespoons vegetable oil, divided
- 3 eggs, lightly beaten
- 1 onion, chopped
- 2 carrots, diced
- 2 cloves garlic, minced
- 1 cup frozen peas, thawed
- 3 green onions, chopped
- Salt and pepper to taste
- Optional garnish: chopped fresh cilantro or parsley

Instructions:

1. Prepare the Shrimp:
    - In a bowl, marinate the shrimp with soy sauce, oyster sauce (if using), and sesame oil. Let it marinate for about 15-20 minutes.
2. Cook the Eggs:
    - Heat 1 tablespoon of vegetable oil in a large skillet or wok over medium heat. Pour the beaten eggs into the skillet and scramble them until they are cooked through. Remove the scrambled eggs from the skillet and set aside.
3. Cook the Shrimp:
    - In the same skillet, heat the remaining tablespoon of vegetable oil over medium-high heat. Add the marinated shrimp and cook for 2-3 minutes on each side, or until they are pink and cooked through. Remove the shrimp from the skillet and set aside.
4. Stir-Fry Vegetables:
    - In the same skillet, add the chopped onion and diced carrots. Cook for 3-4 minutes until they start to soften.
    - Add the minced garlic and cook for an additional minute until fragrant.
5. Combine Rice and Vegetables:

- Add the cooked rice to the skillet with the vegetables. Stir to combine and break up any clumps of rice.
- Add the thawed peas and chopped green onions to the skillet. Stir to incorporate.
6. Add Shrimp and Eggs:
    - Return the cooked shrimp and scrambled eggs to the skillet with the rice and vegetables. Stir to combine and heat through.
7. Season:
    - Season the shrimp fried rice with salt and pepper to taste. Adjust the seasoning if necessary.
8. Serve:
    - Garnish the shrimp fried rice with chopped fresh cilantro or parsley, if desired.
    - Serve hot and enjoy this delicious and satisfying dish!

Shrimp fried rice is a versatile dish, so feel free to customize it by adding other vegetables such as bell peppers, broccoli, or mushrooms. You can also adjust the seasoning to suit your taste preferences. It's a great way to use up leftover rice and makes for a quick and flavorful meal.

Turkey Chili

Ingredients:

- 1 tablespoon olive oil
- 1 onion, chopped
- 1 bell pepper, chopped
- 3 cloves garlic, minced
- 1 pound ground turkey (or leftover cooked turkey, shredded)
- 2 tablespoons chili powder
- 1 teaspoon ground cumin
- 1 teaspoon paprika
- 1/2 teaspoon dried oregano
- 1/2 teaspoon dried thyme
- 1/4 teaspoon cayenne pepper (optional, for added heat)
- Salt and pepper to taste
- 1 can (14.5 ounces) diced tomatoes
- 1 can (15 ounces) tomato sauce
- 1 can (15 ounces) kidney beans, drained and rinsed
- 1 can (15 ounces) black beans, drained and rinsed
- 1 cup corn kernels (fresh, frozen, or canned)
- Optional toppings: shredded cheese, sliced green onions, chopped cilantro, sour cream, avocado

Instructions:

1. Saute Aromatics:
   - Heat the olive oil in a large pot or Dutch oven over medium heat. Add the chopped onion and bell pepper. Cook, stirring occasionally, until softened, about 5-7 minutes.
   - Add the minced garlic and cook for an additional 1-2 minutes until fragrant.
2. Cook the Turkey:
   - Add the ground turkey to the pot. Cook, breaking it up with a spoon, until browned and cooked through. If using leftover cooked turkey, add it at this stage and stir to combine with the aromatics.
3. Season the Chili:
   - Sprinkle the chili powder, ground cumin, paprika, dried oregano, dried thyme, cayenne pepper (if using), salt, and pepper over the turkey mixture. Stir well to coat the turkey and vegetables with the spices.
4. Add Remaining Ingredients:
   - Pour in the diced tomatoes (with their juices), tomato sauce, drained and rinsed kidney beans, drained and rinsed black beans, and corn kernels. Stir to combine.
5. Simmer:
   - Bring the chili to a simmer over medium-low heat. Cover the pot and let it simmer for about 20-30 minutes, stirring occasionally, to allow the flavors to meld together and the chili to thicken to your desired consistency.
6. Adjust Seasoning:
   - Taste the chili and adjust the seasoning with additional salt, pepper, or spices if needed.
7. Serve:
   - Ladle the turkey chili into bowls. Top with your favorite toppings such as shredded cheese, sliced green onions, chopped cilantro, sour cream, or avocado.
   - Serve hot and enjoy this delicious and comforting dish!

Turkey chili is versatile and can be customized according to your taste preferences. Feel free to add extra vegetables like diced carrots, celery, or zucchini for added nutrition and flavor. It's a satisfying meal that's perfect for gatherings or meal prep for busy weekdays.

Chicken Alfredo Pasta Bake

Ingredients:

- 12 ounces fettuccine or penne pasta

- 2 cups cooked chicken, diced or shredded
- 2 tablespoons butter
- 3 cloves garlic, minced
- 2 cups heavy cream
- 1 cup grated Parmesan cheese
- 1 cup shredded mozzarella cheese
- Salt and pepper to taste
- 1/2 teaspoon dried basil
- 1/2 teaspoon dried oregano
- 1/4 teaspoon crushed red pepper flakes (optional)
- Chopped fresh parsley for garnish

Instructions:

1. Preheat the Oven:
    - Preheat your oven to 375°F (190°C). Grease a 9x13-inch baking dish with butter or cooking spray.
2. Cook the Pasta:
    - Cook the fettuccine or penne pasta according to the package instructions until al dente. Drain and set aside.
3. Prepare the Alfredo Sauce:
    - In a large skillet, melt the butter over medium heat. Add the minced garlic and cook for 1-2 minutes until fragrant.
    - Pour in the heavy cream and bring to a simmer. Let it simmer for 3-4 minutes, stirring occasionally.
    - Gradually add the grated Parmesan cheese, stirring constantly until the cheese is melted and the sauce is smooth.
    - Season the Alfredo sauce with salt, pepper, dried basil, dried oregano, and crushed red pepper flakes (if using). Stir to combine.
4. Combine Pasta and Chicken:
    - Add the cooked pasta and diced or shredded chicken to the skillet with the Alfredo sauce. Stir until everything is well coated with the sauce.
5. Assemble the Pasta Bake:
    - Transfer the chicken Alfredo pasta mixture to the prepared baking dish. Spread it out evenly.
    - Sprinkle the shredded mozzarella cheese over the top of the pasta.
6. Bake:
    - Cover the baking dish with aluminum foil and bake in the preheated oven for 20-25 minutes, or until the cheese is melted and bubbly.
    - Remove the foil and bake for an additional 5-10 minutes, or until the cheese is golden brown and the edges are bubbling.
7. Serve:

- Remove the chicken Alfredo pasta bake from the oven and let it cool for a few minutes.
- Garnish with chopped fresh parsley before serving.
- Serve hot and enjoy this creamy and delicious pasta bake!

Chicken Alfredo pasta bake is a crowd-pleaser and can be served with a side salad or garlic bread for a complete meal. It's perfect for sharing with family and friends on special occasions or any night of the week.

Greek Chicken Souvlaki

Ingredients:

For the Chicken Marinade:

- 1.5 pounds boneless, skinless chicken breasts or thighs, cut into bite-sized pieces
- 1/4 cup olive oil
- 3 tablespoons freshly squeezed lemon juice
- 3 cloves garlic, minced
- 1 teaspoon dried oregano
- 1 teaspoon dried thyme
- 1 teaspoon dried rosemary
- 1/2 teaspoon smoked paprika
- Salt and pepper to taste

For Serving:

- Pita bread or flatbread
- Tzatziki sauce
- Sliced tomatoes
- Sliced cucumbers
- Sliced red onions
- Crumbled feta cheese
- Fresh parsley, chopped
- Lemon wedges

Instructions:

1. Marinate the Chicken:

- 2 cups cooked chicken, diced or shredded
- 2 tablespoons butter
- 3 cloves garlic, minced
- 2 cups heavy cream
- 1 cup grated Parmesan cheese
- 1 cup shredded mozzarella cheese
- Salt and pepper to taste
- 1/2 teaspoon dried basil
- 1/2 teaspoon dried oregano
- 1/4 teaspoon crushed red pepper flakes (optional)
- Chopped fresh parsley for garnish

Instructions:

1. Preheat the Oven:
    - Preheat your oven to 375°F (190°C). Grease a 9x13-inch baking dish with butter or cooking spray.
2. Cook the Pasta:
    - Cook the fettuccine or penne pasta according to the package instructions until al dente. Drain and set aside.
3. Prepare the Alfredo Sauce:
    - In a large skillet, melt the butter over medium heat. Add the minced garlic and cook for 1-2 minutes until fragrant.
    - Pour in the heavy cream and bring to a simmer. Let it simmer for 3-4 minutes, stirring occasionally.
    - Gradually add the grated Parmesan cheese, stirring constantly until the cheese is melted and the sauce is smooth.
    - Season the Alfredo sauce with salt, pepper, dried basil, dried oregano, and crushed red pepper flakes (if using). Stir to combine.
4. Combine Pasta and Chicken:
    - Add the cooked pasta and diced or shredded chicken to the skillet with the Alfredo sauce. Stir until everything is well coated with the sauce.
5. Assemble the Pasta Bake:
    - Transfer the chicken Alfredo pasta mixture to the prepared baking dish. Spread it out evenly.
    - Sprinkle the shredded mozzarella cheese over the top of the pasta.
6. Bake:
    - Cover the baking dish with aluminum foil and bake in the preheated oven for 20-25 minutes, or until the cheese is melted and bubbly.
    - Remove the foil and bake for an additional 5-10 minutes, or until the cheese is golden brown and the edges are bubbling.
7. Serve:

- Remove the chicken Alfredo pasta bake from the oven and let it cool for a few minutes.
- Garnish with chopped fresh parsley before serving.
- Serve hot and enjoy this creamy and delicious pasta bake!

Chicken Alfredo pasta bake is a crowd-pleaser and can be served with a side salad or garlic bread for a complete meal. It's perfect for sharing with family and friends on special occasions or any night of the week.

Greek Chicken Souvlaki

Ingredients:

For the Chicken Marinade:

- 1.5 pounds boneless, skinless chicken breasts or thighs, cut into bite-sized pieces
- 1/4 cup olive oil
- 3 tablespoons freshly squeezed lemon juice
- 3 cloves garlic, minced
- 1 teaspoon dried oregano
- 1 teaspoon dried thyme
- 1 teaspoon dried rosemary
- 1/2 teaspoon smoked paprika
- Salt and pepper to taste

For Serving:

- Pita bread or flatbread
- Tzatziki sauce
- Sliced tomatoes
- Sliced cucumbers
- Sliced red onions
- Crumbled feta cheese
- Fresh parsley, chopped
- Lemon wedges

Instructions:

1. Marinate the Chicken:

- In a large bowl, whisk together the olive oil, lemon juice, minced garlic, dried oregano, dried thyme, dried rosemary, smoked paprika, salt, and pepper.
- Add the bite-sized chicken pieces to the marinade and toss until evenly coated. Cover the bowl and refrigerate for at least 30 minutes, or up to 4 hours to allow the flavors to meld together.

2. Prepare the Skewers:
    - If using wooden skewers, soak them in water for at least 30 minutes to prevent burning.
    - Thread the marinated chicken pieces onto the skewers, leaving a little space between each piece.
3. Grill or Cook the Chicken:
    - Preheat your grill or grill pan over medium-high heat. Lightly oil the grates to prevent sticking.
    - Place the chicken skewers on the preheated grill and cook for 6-8 minutes per side, or until the chicken is cooked through and has nice grill marks. Alternatively, you can cook the skewers in a skillet or under the broiler in the oven.
    - Once cooked, remove the chicken skewers from the heat and let them rest for a few minutes.
4. Assemble the Souvlaki:
    - Warm the pita bread or flatbread on the grill or in the oven.
    - Place the grilled chicken from the skewers onto the warmed pita bread.
    - Top with sliced tomatoes, cucumbers, red onions, crumbled feta cheese, and a dollop of tzatziki sauce.
    - Sprinkle with chopped fresh parsley and squeeze fresh lemon juice over the top.
5. Serve:
    - Serve the Greek chicken souvlaki immediately, with extra lemon wedges on the side.
    - Enjoy this delicious and flavorful Mediterranean dish!

Greek chicken souvlaki is perfect for serving as a main course for lunch or dinner. It's also great for outdoor grilling parties or gatherings with friends and family.

Shepherd's Pie

Ingredients:

For the Mashed Potatoes:

- 2 pounds potatoes (such as Russet or Yukon Gold), peeled and cut into chunks
- 4 tablespoons butter
- 1/2 cup milk or cream

- Salt and pepper to taste

For the Filling:

- 1 tablespoon olive oil
- 1 onion, chopped
- 2 carrots, diced
- 2 cloves garlic, minced
- 1 pound ground beef or lamb
- 1 tablespoon tomato paste
- 1 cup beef or vegetable broth
- 1 tablespoon Worcestershire sauce
- 1 teaspoon dried thyme
- 1 teaspoon dried rosemary
- Salt and pepper to taste
- 1 cup frozen peas
- 1 cup frozen corn

Instructions:

1. Make the Mashed Potatoes:
    - Place the potato chunks in a large pot and cover with water. Bring to a boil over high heat, then reduce the heat to medium and simmer for 15-20 minutes, or until the potatoes are fork-tender.
    - Drain the potatoes and return them to the pot. Add the butter and milk or cream. Mash the potatoes until smooth and creamy. Season with salt and pepper to taste. Set aside.
2. Prepare the Filling:
    - Preheat your oven to 400°F (200°C).
    - In a large skillet, heat the olive oil over medium heat. Add the chopped onion and diced carrots. Cook for 5-7 minutes, or until the vegetables are softened.
    - Add the minced garlic and cook for an additional minute until fragrant.
    - Add the ground beef or lamb to the skillet. Cook, breaking it up with a spoon, until browned and cooked through.
    - Stir in the tomato paste, beef or vegetable broth, Worcestershire sauce, dried thyme, dried rosemary, salt, and pepper. Simmer for 5-7 minutes, or until the mixture has thickened slightly.
    - Stir in the frozen peas and corn. Cook for another 2-3 minutes, then remove the skillet from the heat.
3. Assemble the Shepherd's Pie:
    - Transfer the filling mixture to a greased 9x13-inch baking dish, spreading it out evenly.

- Spoon the mashed potatoes over the top of the filling, spreading them out to cover the entire surface.
- Use a fork to create a decorative pattern on the surface of the mashed potatoes, if desired.

4. Bake:
    - Place the baking dish in the preheated oven and bake for 25-30 minutes, or until the mashed potatoes are golden brown and the filling is bubbling around the edges.
5. Serve:
    - Remove the Shepherd's pie from the oven and let it cool for a few minutes before serving.
    - Serve hot and enjoy this comforting and satisfying dish!

Shepherd's pie is perfect for a cozy family dinner and leftovers can be refrigerated and reheated for easy meals throughout the week.

Ratatouille

Ingredients:

- 1 large eggplant, diced
- 2 zucchinis, diced
- 1 yellow bell pepper, diced
- 1 red bell pepper, diced
- 1 onion, diced
- 3 cloves garlic, minced
- 2 large tomatoes, diced
- 2 tablespoons tomato paste
- 2 tablespoons olive oil
- 1 teaspoon dried thyme
- 1 teaspoon dried oregano
- Salt and pepper to taste
- Fresh basil leaves, chopped, for garnish

Instructions:

1. Prepare the Vegetables:
    - Heat 1 tablespoon of olive oil in a large skillet or Dutch oven over medium heat. Add the diced eggplant and cook until softened, about 5-7 minutes. Remove from the skillet and set aside.

- In the same skillet, add another tablespoon of olive oil. Add the diced zucchini, yellow bell pepper, red bell pepper, onion, and minced garlic. Cook, stirring occasionally, until the vegetables are softened, about 7-8 minutes.
2. Combine the Vegetables:
    - Return the cooked eggplant to the skillet with the other vegetables.
    - Add the diced tomatoes and tomato paste to the skillet. Stir to combine.
3. Season:
    - Season the ratatouille with dried thyme, dried oregano, salt, and pepper to taste. Stir well to incorporate the seasoning.
4. Simmer:
    - Reduce the heat to low and let the ratatouille simmer for 20-25 minutes, stirring occasionally, until the vegetables are tender and the flavors have melded together.
5. Serve:
    - Once the ratatouille is cooked to your liking, remove it from the heat.
    - Serve hot, garnished with chopped fresh basil leaves.
    - Ratatouille can be served as a side dish, over cooked rice or pasta, or even on its own as a main course.

Ratatouille is a versatile dish that can be customized based on personal preference. Some variations include adding additional vegetables such as mushrooms, carrots, or celery, or adding fresh herbs like parsley or thyme for extra flavor. Enjoy this classic French dish as a delicious and healthy meal option!

Black Bean and Corn Quesadillas

Ingredients:

- 1 can (15 ounces) black beans, drained and rinsed
- 1 cup corn kernels (fresh, frozen, or canned)
- 1/2 cup diced bell peppers (any color)
- 1/4 cup diced red onion
- 1 teaspoon ground cumin
- 1/2 teaspoon chili powder
- Salt and pepper to taste
- 1 cup shredded cheese (such as cheddar, Monterey Jack, or a Mexican blend)
- 4 large flour tortillas
- Olive oil or cooking spray, for cooking
- Optional toppings: salsa, guacamole, sour cream, chopped cilantro

Instructions:

1. Prepare the Filling:
   - In a mixing bowl, combine the black beans, corn kernels, diced bell peppers, diced red onion, ground cumin, chili powder, salt, and pepper. Stir until well combined.
2. Assemble the Quesadillas:
   - Lay a tortilla flat on a clean work surface. Spread a quarter of the black bean and corn mixture evenly over one half of the tortilla.
   - Sprinkle a quarter of the shredded cheese over the bean mixture.
   - Fold the other half of the tortilla over the filling to create a half-moon shape.
3. Cook the Quesadillas:
   - Heat a large skillet or griddle over medium heat. Lightly brush the surface with olive oil or coat with cooking spray.
   - Carefully place the assembled quesadilla onto the skillet or griddle. Cook for 2-3 minutes on each side, or until the tortilla is golden brown and crispy, and the cheese is melted.
   - Repeat with the remaining tortillas and filling.
4. Serve:
   - Once cooked, transfer the quesadillas to a cutting board and let them cool for a minute.
   - Use a sharp knife to cut each quesadilla into wedges.
   - Serve hot with your favorite toppings such as salsa, guacamole, sour cream, or chopped cilantro.

These black bean and corn quesadillas are customizable, so feel free to add extra ingredients like diced jalapeños, sliced avocado, or cooked chicken or beef if desired. They're perfect for a quick and satisfying meal that's packed with flavor!

Italian Wedding Soup

Ingredients:

For the Meatballs:

- 1/2 pound ground beef
- 1/2 pound ground pork
- 1/2 cup breadcrumbs
- 1/4 cup grated Parmesan cheese
- 1 egg

- 2 cloves garlic, minced
- 1 tablespoon chopped fresh parsley
- Salt and pepper to taste

For the Soup:

- 1 tablespoon olive oil
- 1 onion, chopped
- 2 carrots, diced
- 2 celery stalks, diced
- 8 cups chicken broth
- 1 cup small pasta (such as acini di pepe or small pasta shells)
- 4 cups fresh spinach leaves, chopped
- Salt and pepper to taste
- Grated Parmesan cheese, for serving
- Chopped fresh parsley, for garnish

Instructions:

1. Make the Meatballs:
    - In a large mixing bowl, combine the ground beef, ground pork, breadcrumbs, grated Parmesan cheese, egg, minced garlic, chopped parsley, salt, and pepper. Mix until well combined.
    - Shape the mixture into small meatballs, about 1 inch in diameter. You should get approximately 30-40 meatballs depending on the size.
2. Cook the Meatballs:
    - Heat the olive oil in a large pot or Dutch oven over medium heat. Add the meatballs in batches and cook until browned on all sides, about 5-7 minutes. Remove the meatballs from the pot and set aside.
3. Prepare the Soup:
    - In the same pot, add the chopped onion, diced carrots, and diced celery. Cook, stirring occasionally, until the vegetables are softened, about 5-7 minutes.
    - Pour in the chicken broth and bring the soup to a simmer.
4. Add Pasta and Meatballs:
    - Add the small pasta to the simmering soup. Cook according to the package instructions until the pasta is al dente.
    - Return the cooked meatballs to the pot. Simmer for an additional 5 minutes to heat the meatballs through.
5. Add Spinach and Season:
    - Stir in the chopped fresh spinach leaves and cook for another 1-2 minutes until wilted.
    - Season the soup with salt and pepper to taste.
6. Serve:

- Ladle the Italian wedding soup into bowls. Sprinkle each serving with grated Parmesan cheese and chopped fresh parsley.
- Serve hot and enjoy this comforting and hearty soup!

Italian wedding soup is a delicious and satisfying meal on its own, or you can serve it with crusty bread or a side salad for a complete meal. It's perfect for warming up on chilly days and is sure to be a hit with the whole family!

Lemon Garlic Shrimp

Ingredients:

- 1 pound large shrimp, peeled and deveined
- 3 tablespoons olive oil
- 4 cloves garlic, minced
- Zest of 1 lemon
- Juice of 1 lemon
- 2 tablespoons chopped fresh parsley
- Salt and pepper to taste
- Lemon wedges, for serving
- Cooked rice, pasta, or crusty bread, for serving (optional)

Instructions:

1. Prepare the Shrimp:
    - Pat the shrimp dry with paper towels and season with salt and pepper.
2. Cook the Shrimp:
    - Heat the olive oil in a large skillet over medium-high heat.
    - Add the minced garlic to the skillet and cook for 1-2 minutes until fragrant, being careful not to burn it.
    - Add the seasoned shrimp to the skillet in a single layer. Cook for 2-3 minutes on one side until pink and opaque.
    - Flip the shrimp and cook for an additional 2-3 minutes on the other side until cooked through.
3. Add Lemon and Parsley:
    - Once the shrimp is cooked, add the lemon zest, lemon juice, and chopped fresh parsley to the skillet. Stir to combine and coat the shrimp with the lemon garlic sauce.
4. Serve:

- Remove the skillet from the heat.
- Serve the lemon garlic shrimp hot, garnished with additional chopped parsley and lemon wedges.
- You can serve the shrimp over cooked rice, pasta, or with crusty bread to soak up the delicious sauce.

Lemon garlic shrimp is a versatile dish that can be served as an appetizer, main course, or even as part of a pasta dish or salad. It's bursting with fresh flavors and is sure to be a hit at any meal!

Beef and Mushroom Stroganoff

Ingredients:

- 1 pound beef sirloin or tenderloin, thinly sliced
- Salt and pepper to taste
- 2 tablespoons olive oil
- 8 ounces mushrooms, sliced (button or cremini)
- 1 onion, diced
- 2 cloves garlic, minced
- 2 tablespoons all-purpose flour
- 1 cup beef broth
- 1 cup sour cream
- 1 tablespoon Dijon mustard
- 1 tablespoon Worcestershire sauce
- 1 tablespoon chopped fresh parsley, for garnish
- Cooked egg noodles, rice, or mashed potatoes, for serving

Instructions:

1. Prepare the Beef:
    - Season the thinly sliced beef with salt and pepper to taste.
2. Cook the Beef:
    - Heat 1 tablespoon of olive oil in a large skillet over medium-high heat.
    - Add the seasoned beef to the skillet and cook until browned on all sides, about 3-4 minutes. Remove the beef from the skillet and set aside.

3. Cook the Mushrooms and Onions:
   - In the same skillet, add the remaining tablespoon of olive oil.
   - Add the sliced mushrooms and diced onion to the skillet. Cook, stirring occasionally, until the mushrooms are browned and the onions are softened, about 5-7 minutes.
   - Add the minced garlic to the skillet and cook for an additional minute until fragrant.
4. Make the Sauce:
   - Sprinkle the flour over the mushrooms and onions in the skillet. Stir to combine and cook for 1-2 minutes to cook off the raw flour taste.
   - Gradually pour in the beef broth, stirring constantly to prevent lumps from forming.
   - Bring the mixture to a simmer and cook for 2-3 minutes, or until the sauce has thickened slightly.
5. Finish the Dish:
   - Return the cooked beef to the skillet. Stir in the sour cream, Dijon mustard, and Worcestershire sauce until well combined.
   - Cook for an additional 2-3 minutes, or until the beef is heated through and the sauce is creamy and smooth.
   - Taste and adjust seasoning with salt and pepper if needed.
6. Serve:
   - Serve the beef and mushroom stroganoff hot, garnished with chopped fresh parsley.
   - Serve over cooked egg noodles, rice, or mashed potatoes.

Beef and mushroom stroganoff is a comforting and satisfying dish that's perfect for a cozy dinner at home. Enjoy its rich and creamy flavors!

Sweet and Sour Meatballs

Ingredients:

For the Meatballs:

- 1 pound ground beef
- 1/2 cup breadcrumbs
- 1/4 cup milk

- 1 egg
- 2 cloves garlic, minced
- 1 tablespoon soy sauce
- 1 teaspoon Worcestershire sauce
- Salt and pepper to taste

For the Sauce:

- 1 tablespoon olive oil
- 1 onion, chopped
- 1 bell pepper, chopped (any color)
- 1 can (20 ounces) pineapple chunks in juice, drained (reserve juice)
- 1/2 cup ketchup
- 1/4 cup brown sugar
- 1/4 cup apple cider vinegar
- 2 tablespoons soy sauce
- 1 tablespoon cornstarch
- Cooked rice or noodles, for serving
- Chopped green onions or sesame seeds, for garnish (optional)

Instructions:

1. Make the Meatballs:
   - Preheat your oven to 400°F (200°C). Line a baking sheet with parchment paper or aluminum foil.
   - In a large mixing bowl, combine the ground beef, breadcrumbs, milk, egg, minced garlic, soy sauce, Worcestershire sauce, salt, and pepper. Mix until well combined.
   - Shape the mixture into meatballs, about 1 inch in diameter. Place them on the prepared baking sheet.
   - Bake in the preheated oven for 15-20 minutes, or until the meatballs are cooked through and browned.
2. Prepare the Sauce:
   - In a large skillet or saucepan, heat the olive oil over medium heat. Add the chopped onion and bell pepper. Cook, stirring occasionally, until the vegetables are softened, about 5-7 minutes.
   - Add the drained pineapple chunks to the skillet and cook for another 2-3 minutes.
   - In a small bowl, whisk together the ketchup, brown sugar, apple cider vinegar, soy sauce, and 1/4 cup of the reserved pineapple juice. Stir the sauce into the skillet with the vegetables and pineapple.
3. Thicken the Sauce:
   - In a separate small bowl, mix the cornstarch with 2 tablespoons of water to create a slurry.

- Stir the cornstarch slurry into the skillet with the sauce. Cook, stirring constantly, until the sauce has thickened slightly, about 2-3 minutes.
4. Combine the Meatballs and Sauce:
    - Add the baked meatballs to the skillet with the sweet and sour sauce. Gently toss to coat the meatballs in the sauce.
5. Serve:
    - Serve the sweet and sour meatballs hot over cooked rice or noodles.
    - Garnish with chopped green onions or sesame seeds, if desired.

Sweet and sour meatballs are a crowd-pleasing dish that's perfect for family dinners or potlucks. Enjoy the delicious combination of flavors!

Chicken Curry

Ingredients:

- 1.5 pounds boneless, skinless chicken thighs or breasts, cut into bite-sized pieces
- 2 tablespoons vegetable oil or ghee
- 1 large onion, finely chopped
- 3 cloves garlic, minced
- 1-inch piece of ginger, grated or minced
- 2 tablespoons curry powder
- 1 teaspoon ground turmeric
- 1 teaspoon ground cumin
- 1 teaspoon ground coriander
- 1/2 teaspoon chili powder (adjust to taste)
- 1 can (14 ounces) diced tomatoes
- 1 can (13.5 ounces) coconut milk
- Salt and pepper to taste
- Fresh cilantro leaves, chopped, for garnish
- Cooked rice or naan bread, for serving

Instructions:

1. Cook the Chicken:

- Heat the vegetable oil or ghee in a large skillet or Dutch oven over medium heat.
- Add the chopped onion and cook until softened, about 5 minutes.
- Add the minced garlic and grated ginger, and cook for another 1-2 minutes until fragrant.
- Add the chicken pieces to the skillet and cook until browned on all sides, about 5-7 minutes.
2. Make the Curry Sauce:
    - Sprinkle the curry powder, ground turmeric, ground cumin, ground coriander, and chili powder over the chicken. Stir to coat the chicken in the spices.
    - Pour in the diced tomatoes and coconut milk. Stir to combine.
    - Season with salt and pepper to taste.
3. Simmer the Curry:
    - Bring the mixture to a simmer, then reduce the heat to low. Cover and let the curry simmer gently for 20-25 minutes, stirring occasionally, until the chicken is cooked through and the sauce has thickened.
4. Serve:
    - Once the chicken curry is cooked to your liking, remove it from the heat.
    - Serve the chicken curry hot over cooked rice or with naan bread.
    - Garnish with chopped fresh cilantro leaves before serving.

Chicken curry is a versatile dish, and you can customize it by adding vegetables like bell peppers, potatoes, or peas. Adjust the spices according to your taste preferences, adding more chili powder for heat or more curry powder for a stronger flavor. Enjoy this delicious and comforting dish!

Cheesy Broccoli Rice Casserole

Ingredients:

- 2 cups broccoli florets
- 1 cup uncooked long-grain white rice
- 2 cups chicken or vegetable broth
- 1 tablespoon butter
- 1 small onion, diced

- 2 cloves garlic, minced
- 2 tablespoons all-purpose flour
- 1 cup milk
- 2 cups shredded cheddar cheese
- Salt and pepper to taste
- 1/4 cup grated Parmesan cheese
- 1/2 cup breadcrumbs (optional)
- Cooking spray or butter, for greasing the baking dish

Instructions:

1. Cook the Rice and Broccoli:
    - Preheat your oven to 350°F (175°C). Grease a 9x13-inch baking dish with cooking spray or butter.
    - In a medium saucepan, bring the chicken or vegetable broth to a boil. Stir in the rice, reduce the heat to low, cover, and simmer for 15-20 minutes, or until the rice is cooked and the broth is absorbed.
    - Steam the broccoli florets until tender, about 5-7 minutes. Drain and set aside.
2. Make the Cheese Sauce:
    - In a large skillet, melt the butter over medium heat. Add the diced onion and minced garlic, and cook until softened, about 3-4 minutes.
    - Sprinkle the flour over the onion and garlic, and cook for an additional 1-2 minutes, stirring constantly.
    - Gradually whisk in the milk, stirring constantly to prevent lumps from forming. Cook until the sauce thickens, about 3-4 minutes.
    - Stir in the shredded cheddar cheese until melted and smooth. Season with salt and pepper to taste.
3. Assemble the Casserole:
    - In the prepared baking dish, combine the cooked rice, steamed broccoli, and cheese sauce. Stir until well combined.
    - Sprinkle the grated Parmesan cheese evenly over the top of the casserole. If desired, sprinkle breadcrumbs over the Parmesan cheese for extra crunch.
4. Bake the Casserole:
    - Cover the baking dish with aluminum foil and bake in the preheated oven for 20-25 minutes.
    - Remove the foil and bake for an additional 5-10 minutes, or until the casserole is heated through and bubbly, and the top is golden brown.
5. Serve:
    - Remove the cheesy broccoli rice casserole from the oven and let it cool for a few minutes before serving.
    - Serve hot as a comforting side dish or a satisfying vegetarian main course.

This cheesy broccoli rice casserole is perfect for family dinners, potlucks, or holiday gatherings. Enjoy its creamy and comforting flavors!

Pork Carnitas

Ingredients:

- 3-4 pounds pork shoulder (also known as pork butt), trimmed of excess fat and cut into large chunks
- 1 onion, quartered
- 4 cloves garlic, smashed
- 2 bay leaves
- 1 tablespoon ground cumin
- 1 tablespoon dried oregano
- 1 teaspoon smoked paprika
- 1 teaspoon ground coriander
- 1 teaspoon chili powder
- 1 teaspoon salt, or to taste
- 1/2 teaspoon black pepper, or to taste
- 1 orange, juiced
- 1 lime, juiced
- 2 tablespoons vegetable oil or lard
- Fresh cilantro, chopped (for garnish)
- Lime wedges (for serving)
- Corn or flour tortillas, for serving

Instructions:

1. Marinate the Pork:
    - In a large bowl or resealable plastic bag, combine the pork shoulder chunks, quartered onion, smashed garlic cloves, bay leaves, ground cumin, dried oregano, smoked paprika, ground coriander, chili powder, salt, pepper, orange juice, and lime juice. Mix well to coat the pork evenly. Marinate in the refrigerator for at least 2 hours, preferably overnight.
2. Slow Cook the Pork:
    - Preheat your oven to 325°F (160°C).
    - Transfer the marinated pork and aromatics to a large Dutch oven or oven-safe pot. Cover with a lid or aluminum foil.
    - Place the pot in the preheated oven and cook for 3-4 hours, or until the pork is very tender and easily shreds with a fork.
3. Shred the Pork:

- Once the pork is cooked, remove it from the oven and use two forks to shred it into smaller pieces. Discard any large pieces of fat or gristle.
4. Crisp the Pork:
    - Heat the vegetable oil or lard in a large skillet or frying pan over medium-high heat.
    - Add the shredded pork in batches, spreading it out in an even layer. Let it cook without stirring for 3-5 minutes, or until the bottom is crispy and golden brown.
    - Use a spatula to flip the pork and crisp up the other side, another 3-5 minutes. Repeat with the remaining pork.
5. Serve:
    - Once all the pork is crispy and golden brown, transfer it to a serving platter.
    - Garnish with chopped fresh cilantro and serve hot with lime wedges and warm tortillas.

Pork carnitas are delicious served with your favorite toppings such as salsa, diced onions, chopped cilantro, guacamole, or shredded cheese. Enjoy them as tacos, burritos, nachos, or simply with rice and beans for a flavorful meal!

Minestrone Soup

Ingredients:

- 2 tablespoons olive oil
- 1 onion, chopped
- 2 cloves garlic, minced
- 2 carrots, diced
- 2 celery stalks, diced
- 1 zucchini, diced
- 1 yellow squash, diced
- 1 bell pepper, diced (any color)
- 1 can (14 ounces) diced tomatoes
- 1 can (15 ounces) kidney beans, drained and rinsed
- 1 can (15 ounces) cannellini beans, drained and rinsed
- 6 cups vegetable broth or chicken broth
- 1 teaspoon dried oregano
- 1 teaspoon dried basil
- 1 teaspoon dried thyme
- 1 teaspoon dried rosemary

- Salt and pepper to taste
- 1 cup small pasta (such as ditalini or small shells)
- 2 cups fresh spinach leaves, chopped
- Grated Parmesan cheese, for serving
- Fresh basil leaves, chopped, for garnish

Instructions:

1. Sauté the Vegetables:
    - In a large soup pot or Dutch oven, heat the olive oil over medium heat. Add the chopped onion and minced garlic, and cook until softened and fragrant, about 3-4 minutes.
    - Add the diced carrots, celery, zucchini, yellow squash, and bell pepper to the pot. Cook, stirring occasionally, for another 5-7 minutes, or until the vegetables are slightly softened.
2. Add Tomatoes, Beans, and Broth:
    - Stir in the diced tomatoes, kidney beans, cannellini beans, vegetable broth, dried oregano, dried basil, dried thyme, dried rosemary, salt, and pepper.
    - Bring the soup to a simmer, then reduce the heat to low. Cover and let the soup simmer for about 20-25 minutes to allow the flavors to meld together.
3. Cook the Pasta:
    - While the soup is simmering, cook the pasta in a separate pot according to the package instructions until al dente. Drain and set aside.
4. Finish the Soup:
    - Once the soup has simmered and the vegetables are tender, stir in the cooked pasta and chopped fresh spinach leaves.
    - Let the soup cook for an additional 2-3 minutes, or until the spinach wilts and the pasta is heated through.
    - Taste and adjust the seasoning with salt and pepper if needed.
5. Serve:
    - Ladle the minestrone soup into bowls. Sprinkle each serving with grated Parmesan cheese and chopped fresh basil leaves.
    - Serve hot and enjoy this hearty and flavorful Italian soup!

Minestrone soup is perfect for a comforting meal on a chilly day, and it's even better the next day as the flavors continue to develop. Serve it with crusty bread or a side salad for a complete and satisfying meal.

Spaghetti Bolognese

Ingredients:

For the Bolognese Sauce:

- 1 tablespoon olive oil
- 1 onion, finely chopped
- 2 cloves garlic, minced
- 1 carrot, finely chopped
- 1 celery stalk, finely chopped
- 1 pound ground beef (or a mix of beef and pork)
- 1 can (14 ounces) diced tomatoes
- 1/2 cup tomato paste
- 1 cup beef broth
- 1 teaspoon dried oregano
- 1 teaspoon dried basil
- 1/2 teaspoon dried thyme
- Salt and pepper to taste
- 1/4 cup red wine (optional)
- Grated Parmesan cheese, for serving

For the Spaghetti:

- 1 pound spaghetti noodles
- Salt for pasta water
- Fresh parsley, chopped (for garnish)

Instructions:

1. Prepare the Bolognese Sauce:
    - Heat the olive oil in a large skillet or Dutch oven over medium heat. Add the chopped onion, minced garlic, chopped carrot, and chopped celery.

Cook, stirring occasionally, until the vegetables are softened, about 5-7 minutes.
- Add the ground beef to the skillet. Cook, breaking it up with a spoon, until browned and cooked through.
- Stir in the diced tomatoes, tomato paste, beef broth, dried oregano, dried basil, dried thyme, salt, and pepper. If using red wine, add it now.
- Bring the sauce to a simmer, then reduce the heat to low. Let it simmer uncovered for at least 30 minutes (or up to 2 hours), stirring occasionally, to allow the flavors to meld together and the sauce to thicken. If the sauce becomes too thick, you can add a little more beef broth or water.

2. Cook the Spaghetti:
   - While the sauce is simmering, bring a large pot of salted water to a boil. Cook the spaghetti noodles according to the package instructions until al dente.
   - Drain the cooked spaghetti and return it to the pot.

3. Combine the Sauce and Spaghetti:
   - Once the Bolognese sauce is ready, pour it over the cooked spaghetti noodles in the pot. Toss gently to combine, ensuring the noodles are well coated with the sauce.

4. Serve:
   - Divide the spaghetti Bolognese among serving plates or bowls. Sprinkle each serving with grated Parmesan cheese and chopped fresh parsley.
   - Serve hot and enjoy this classic Italian pasta dish!

Spaghetti Bolognese is delicious on its own, but you can also serve it with garlic bread or a side salad for a complete and satisfying meal. Enjoy!

Chicken Cacciatore**Ingredients:**

- 4 bone-in, skin-on chicken thighs
- 4 bone-in, skin-on chicken drumsticks
- Salt and pepper to taste
- 2 tablespoons olive oil
- 1 onion, chopped
- 2 cloves garlic, minced
- 1 bell pepper, sliced (any color)
- 1 carrot, diced
- 8 ounces mushrooms, sliced
- 1 can (14 ounces) diced tomatoes

- 1/2 cup chicken broth
- 1/4 cup dry white wine (optional)
- 2 tablespoons tomato paste
- 1 teaspoon dried oregano
- 1 teaspoon dried basil
- 1/2 teaspoon dried thyme
- 1 bay leaf
- Chopped fresh parsley, for garnish

Instructions:

1. Season and Brown the Chicken:
   - Season the chicken thighs and drumsticks generously with salt and pepper.
   - Heat the olive oil in a large skillet or Dutch oven over medium-high heat. Add the chicken pieces, skin-side down, and cook until golden brown, about 5-7 minutes per side. Remove the chicken from the skillet and set aside.
2. Sauté the Vegetables:
   - In the same skillet, add the chopped onion, minced garlic, sliced bell pepper, diced carrot, and sliced mushrooms. Cook, stirring occasionally, until the vegetables are softened, about 5-7 minutes.
3. Simmer the Sauce:
   - Stir in the diced tomatoes, chicken broth, dry white wine (if using), tomato paste, dried oregano, dried basil, dried thyme, and bay leaf.
   - Return the browned chicken pieces to the skillet, nestling them into the sauce.
   - Bring the mixture to a simmer, then reduce the heat to low. Cover and let the chicken cacciatore simmer for about 30-40 minutes, or until the chicken is cooked through and tender, and the sauce has thickened.
4. Serve:
   - Once the chicken cacciatore is cooked, remove the bay leaf.
   - Serve the chicken cacciatore hot, garnished with chopped fresh parsley.
   - You can serve it over cooked pasta, rice, or polenta, or with crusty bread to soak up the delicious sauce.

Chicken cacciatore is a flavorful and comforting dish that's perfect for a family dinner or entertaining guests. Enjoy its rich and hearty flavors!

Beef Burritos

Ingredients:

For the Beef Filling:

- 1 pound ground beef
- 1 small onion, finely chopped
- 2 cloves garlic, minced
- 1 tablespoon chili powder
- 1 teaspoon ground cumin
- 1/2 teaspoon paprika
- 1/2 teaspoon dried oregano
- Salt and pepper to taste
- 1 can (14 ounces) black beans, drained and rinsed

For Assembling the Burritos:

- Large flour tortillas
- Cooked rice
- Shredded cheese (such as cheddar or Monterey Jack)
- Diced tomatoes
- Chopped lettuce
- Sliced avocado or guacamole
- Sour cream
- Salsa
- Chopped fresh cilantro (optional)
- Lime wedges (optional)

Instructions:

1. Cook the Beef Filling:
   - In a large skillet, cook the ground beef over medium heat until browned and cooked through, breaking it up with a spoon as it cooks.
   - Add the chopped onion and minced garlic to the skillet with the beef. Cook for an additional 2-3 minutes, until the onion is softened.
   - Stir in the chili powder, ground cumin, paprika, dried oregano, salt, and pepper. Cook for another 1-2 minutes to toast the spices.
   - Add the drained and rinsed black beans to the skillet. Stir to combine and cook for a few more minutes until heated through. Remove from heat.
2. Assemble the Burritos:
   - Warm the flour tortillas in a dry skillet or in the microwave for a few seconds to make them pliable.
   - Place a spoonful of cooked rice in the center of each tortilla, followed by a spoonful of the beef and bean mixture.
   - Top with shredded cheese, diced tomatoes, chopped lettuce, sliced avocado or guacamole, sour cream, salsa, and any other desired toppings.

3. Fold the Burritos:
    - Fold the sides of the tortilla over the filling, then fold the bottom edge up and over the filling, tucking it tightly.
    - Continue rolling the burrito until it is tightly wrapped.
4. Serve:
    - Serve the beef burritos immediately, or wrap them in foil and keep them warm in a low oven until ready to serve.
    - Optionally, garnish with chopped fresh cilantro and serve with lime wedges on the side.

Beef burritos are customizable, so feel free to add or omit any ingredients based on your preferences. They make a delicious and satisfying meal that's perfect for lunch or dinner!

Creamy Tomato Tortellini Soup

Ingredients:

- 1 tablespoon olive oil
- 1 small onion, finely chopped
- 2 cloves garlic, minced
- 1 can (14 ounces) crushed tomatoes
- 4 cups chicken or vegetable broth
- 1 teaspoon dried basil
- 1 teaspoon dried oregano
- 1/2 teaspoon dried thyme
- 1/2 teaspoon crushed red pepper flakes (optional, for heat)
- Salt and pepper to taste
- 1 cup heavy cream
- 1 package (9 ounces) refrigerated cheese tortellini
- Fresh basil leaves, chopped, for garnish
- Grated Parmesan cheese, for serving

Instructions:

1. Sauté the Aromatics:

- Heat the olive oil in a large pot or Dutch oven over medium heat. Add the chopped onion and minced garlic, and sauté until softened and fragrant, about 3-4 minutes.
2. Make the Soup Base:
    - Add the crushed tomatoes, chicken or vegetable broth, dried basil, dried oregano, dried thyme, crushed red pepper flakes (if using), salt, and pepper to the pot. Stir to combine.
    - Bring the soup to a simmer, then reduce the heat to low. Let it simmer gently for about 15-20 minutes to allow the flavors to meld together.
3. Cook the Tortellini:
    - While the soup is simmering, cook the cheese tortellini according to the package instructions until al dente. Drain and set aside.
4. Add Cream:
    - Once the soup has simmered and the flavors have developed, stir in the heavy cream. Taste and adjust seasoning with salt and pepper if needed.
5. Combine Soup and Tortellini:
    - Add the cooked cheese tortellini to the pot of creamy tomato soup. Stir gently to combine, ensuring the tortellini are evenly distributed in the soup.
6. Serve:
    - Ladle the creamy tomato tortellini soup into bowls. Garnish with chopped fresh basil leaves and grated Parmesan cheese.
    - Serve hot and enjoy this comforting and satisfying soup!

Creamy tomato tortellini soup is perfect for a cozy dinner on a cold evening. Serve it with crusty bread or a side salad for a complete meal. It's sure to be a hit with the whole family!

Veggie-Packed Bolognese Sauce

Ingredients:

- 2 tablespoons olive oil
- 1 onion, finely chopped
- 2 carrots, finely chopped
- 2 celery stalks, finely chopped
- 1 bell pepper, finely chopped (any color)
- 8 ounces mushrooms, finely chopped
- 3 cloves garlic, minced

- 1 zucchini, grated
- 1 cup cooked lentils (optional, for extra protein)
- 1 can (14 ounces) crushed tomatoes
- 1 can (6 ounces) tomato paste
- 1 cup vegetable broth
- 1 teaspoon dried oregano
- 1 teaspoon dried basil
- 1/2 teaspoon dried thyme
- Salt and pepper to taste
- 1 bay leaf
- Cooked pasta of your choice, for serving
- Grated Parmesan cheese, for serving
- Chopped fresh parsley, for garnish

Instructions:

1. Sauté the Vegetables:
   - Heat the olive oil in a large skillet or Dutch oven over medium heat. Add the chopped onion, carrots, celery, bell pepper, mushrooms, and grated zucchini. Cook, stirring occasionally, until the vegetables are softened, about 8-10 minutes.
2. Add Garlic and Lentils:
   - Add the minced garlic to the skillet with the sautéed vegetables. Cook for another 1-2 minutes until fragrant.
   - If using cooked lentils for extra protein, add them to the skillet now and stir to combine with the vegetables.
3. Make the Sauce:
   - Stir in the crushed tomatoes, tomato paste, vegetable broth, dried oregano, dried basil, dried thyme, salt, pepper, and bay leaf. Mix well to combine.
   - Bring the sauce to a simmer, then reduce the heat to low. Cover and let it simmer gently for about 30-40 minutes, stirring occasionally, to allow the flavors to meld together and the sauce to thicken.
4. Serve:
   - Once the veggie-packed Bolognese sauce is cooked to your liking, remove the bay leaf.
   - Serve the sauce over cooked pasta of your choice.
   - Garnish with grated Parmesan cheese and chopped fresh parsley before serving.

Veggie-packed Bolognese sauce is a nutritious and satisfying meal that's perfect for vegetarians and meat-lovers alike. Enjoy its rich flavors and hearty texture!

Hawaiian Chicken

Ingredients:

- 4 boneless, skinless chicken breasts
- Salt and pepper to taste
- 1 cup pineapple juice
- 1/4 cup soy sauce
- 1/4 cup ketchup
- 2 tablespoons brown sugar
- 2 cloves garlic, minced
- 1 teaspoon grated fresh ginger
- 1 tablespoon cornstarch
- 1/4 cup water
- Sliced pineapple rings (fresh or canned), for serving
- Cooked rice, for serving
- Chopped green onions or sesame seeds, for garnish (optional)

Instructions:

1. Prepare the Chicken:
    - Season the chicken breasts with salt and pepper on both sides.
2. Make the Sauce:
    - In a small bowl, whisk together the pineapple juice, soy sauce, ketchup, brown sugar, minced garlic, and grated ginger.
    - In a separate small bowl, mix the cornstarch with water to create a slurry.
3. Cook the Chicken:
    - Heat a large skillet or grill pan over medium-high heat. Add the chicken breasts and cook for 4-5 minutes on each side, or until golden brown and cooked through.
    - Remove the chicken from the skillet and set aside.
4. Simmer the Sauce:
    - Pour the pineapple juice mixture into the skillet. Bring to a simmer over medium heat, scraping up any browned bits from the bottom of the pan.
    - Stir in the cornstarch slurry and continue to simmer for 2-3 minutes, or until the sauce has thickened slightly.
5. Combine Chicken and Sauce:

- Return the cooked chicken breasts to the skillet, turning them to coat in the sauce.
- Add the sliced pineapple rings to the skillet, placing them on top of the chicken breasts.

6. Serve:
   - Serve the Hawaiian chicken hot over cooked rice.
   - Garnish with chopped green onions or sesame seeds, if desired.

Hawaiian chicken is a delightful dish that's perfect for a taste of the tropics at home. Enjoy the sweet and savory flavors with a side of rice and some steamed vegetables for a complete meal!

Macaroni and Cheese

Ingredients:

- 8 ounces (about 2 cups) elbow macaroni or any pasta shape of your choice
- 1/4 cup unsalted butter
- 1/4 cup all-purpose flour
- 2 cups whole milk
- 2 cups shredded cheese (such as sharp cheddar, mozzarella, or a combination)
- 1/2 teaspoon salt, or to taste
- 1/4 teaspoon black pepper, or to taste
- Optional toppings: breadcrumbs, additional shredded cheese, chopped fresh herbs

Instructions:

1. Cook the Pasta:
   - Bring a large pot of salted water to a boil. Add the pasta and cook according to the package instructions until al dente. Drain the cooked pasta and set aside.
2. Make the Cheese Sauce:
   - In the same pot (or a separate saucepan), melt the butter over medium heat. Once melted, whisk in the flour to create a roux. Cook the roux, stirring constantly, for 1-2 minutes until lightly golden.
   - Gradually pour in the milk, whisking constantly to prevent lumps from forming. Cook the mixture, stirring frequently, until it thickens and comes to a simmer.
   - Reduce the heat to low and stir in the shredded cheese until melted and smooth. Season with salt and pepper to taste.
3. Combine Pasta and Cheese Sauce:

- Add the cooked pasta to the pot of cheese sauce. Stir gently until the pasta is evenly coated with the sauce.
4. Optional Baking:
    - If you prefer baked macaroni and cheese, transfer the mixture to a greased baking dish. Top with breadcrumbs and additional shredded cheese, if desired.
    - Bake in a preheated 350°F (175°C) oven for 20-25 minutes, or until bubbly and golden brown on top.
5. Serve:
    - Serve the macaroni and cheese hot, straight from the pot or baking dish.
    - Garnish with chopped fresh herbs, if desired.

Macaroni and cheese is a versatile dish, and you can customize it by adding ingredients like cooked bacon, diced ham, broccoli, or diced tomatoes. Enjoy this comforting and cheesy dish as a side or main course!

Moroccan Tagine

Ingredients:

- 1 ½ pounds (about 700g) lamb shoulder, cut into chunks
- 2 tablespoons olive oil
- 1 large onion, chopped
- 2 cloves garlic, minced
- 1 teaspoon ground cumin
- 1 teaspoon ground coriander
- 1 teaspoon ground cinnamon
- ½ teaspoon ground ginger
- ½ teaspoon paprika
- ½ teaspoon turmeric
- ½ teaspoon black pepper
- 1 teaspoon salt, or to taste
- 1 cup (240ml) chicken or vegetable broth
- 1 can (14 oz or 400g) diced tomatoes
- 1 cup (about 150g) dried apricots, chopped
- 1 cup (about 150g) pitted green olives
- 2 tablespoons honey
- Chopped fresh cilantro or parsley, for garnish

Instructions:

1. Heat the olive oil in a large tagine pot or a Dutch oven over medium heat.
2. Add the chopped onion and cook until softened, about 5 minutes. Add the minced garlic and cook for another minute until fragrant.
3. Add the lamb chunks to the pot and brown them on all sides, about 5 minutes.
4. Stir in the ground cumin, coriander, cinnamon, ginger, paprika, turmeric, black pepper, and salt. Cook for 1-2 minutes until the spices are fragrant.
5. Pour in the chicken or vegetable broth and diced tomatoes with their juices. Stir well to combine.
6. Add the chopped dried apricots and green olives to the pot.
7. Bring the mixture to a simmer, then reduce the heat to low. Cover the pot with the tagine lid or a tight-fitting lid if using a Dutch oven.
8. Let the tagine simmer gently for 1.5 to 2 hours, stirring occasionally, or until the lamb is tender and the sauce has thickened.
9. Stir in the honey, taste and adjust seasoning if needed.
10. Garnish with chopped fresh cilantro or parsley before serving.
11. Serve the tagine hot with couscous, rice, or crusty bread.

Enjoy your Moroccan Lamb Tagine!

Sloppy Joes

Ingredients:

- 1 pound (about 450g) ground beef or turkey
- 1 small onion, finely chopped
- 1 small green bell pepper, finely chopped
- 2 cloves garlic, minced
- 1 cup (240ml) ketchup
- 2 tablespoons tomato paste
- 1 tablespoon brown sugar
- 1 tablespoon Worcestershire sauce
- 1 tablespoon apple cider vinegar
- 1 teaspoon mustard
- 1/2 teaspoon chili powder (optional, for a bit of heat)
- Salt and black pepper, to taste
- Hamburger buns, for serving

Instructions:

1. In a large skillet or frying pan, cook the ground beef or turkey over medium heat until browned, breaking it up with a spoon as it cooks. Drain off excess fat if needed.
2. Add the chopped onion and green bell pepper to the skillet with the cooked meat. Cook for 3-4 minutes, until the vegetables are softened.
3. Add the minced garlic to the skillet and cook for another minute, until fragrant.
4. Stir in the ketchup, tomato paste, brown sugar, Worcestershire sauce, apple cider vinegar, mustard, and chili powder (if using) until well combined.
5. Season with salt and black pepper to taste. Reduce the heat to low and let the mixture simmer for 10-15 minutes, stirring occasionally, to allow the flavors to meld together and the sauce to thicken.
6. Once the Sloppy Joe mixture has thickened to your desired consistency, remove the skillet from the heat.
7. Toast the hamburger buns if desired, then spoon the Sloppy Joe mixture onto the bottom halves of the buns.
8. Top with the other half of the buns and serve hot.

Enjoy your homemade Sloppy Joes! They're perfect for a quick and tasty meal, whether for lunch or dinner.

Vegetable Curry

Ingredients:

- 2 tablespoons vegetable oil
- 1 onion, finely chopped
- 2 cloves garlic, minced
- 1 tablespoon ginger, grated
- 2 teaspoons curry powder
- 1 teaspoon ground cumin
- 1 teaspoon ground coriander
- 1/2 teaspoon turmeric
- 1/4 teaspoon cayenne pepper (adjust to taste)
- Salt to taste
- 1 can (14 oz or 400g) diced tomatoes
- 1 can (14 oz or 400ml) coconut milk
- 3 cups mixed vegetables (such as carrots, potatoes, bell peppers, peas, cauliflower, and/or green beans), chopped into bite-sized pieces
- Fresh cilantro leaves, chopped (for garnish)
- Cooked rice or naan bread, for serving

Instructions:

1. Heat the vegetable oil in a large skillet or pot over medium heat.
2. Add the chopped onion and cook until softened, about 5 minutes.
3. Stir in the minced garlic and grated ginger, and cook for another minute until fragrant.
4. Add the curry powder, ground cumin, ground coriander, turmeric, cayenne pepper, and salt to the skillet. Stir well to coat the onions with the spices.
5. Pour in the diced tomatoes with their juices, and stir to combine.
6. Add the chopped vegetables to the skillet, stirring to coat them with the tomato and spice mixture.
7. Pour in the coconut milk, stirring well to combine. Bring the mixture to a simmer.
8. Reduce the heat to low, cover the skillet, and let the curry simmer gently for 15-20 minutes, or until the vegetables are tender.
9. Taste the curry and adjust the seasoning if needed, adding more salt or spices as desired.
10. Once the vegetables are cooked to your liking and the curry has reached your desired consistency, remove the skillet from the heat.
11. Serve the vegetable curry hot, garnished with fresh cilantro leaves, and accompanied by cooked rice or naan bread.

Enjoy your homemade vegetable curry! It's a comforting and satisfying meal that's perfect for vegetarians and meat-eaters alike.

Chicken Tetrazzini

Ingredients:

- 8 ounces (about 225g) spaghetti or fettuccine pasta
- 2 cups diced cooked chicken (rotisserie chicken works well)
- 8 ounces (about 225g) sliced mushrooms
- 1/4 cup (about 55g) unsalted butter
- 1/4 cup (about 30g) all-purpose flour
- 2 cups chicken broth
- 1 cup whole milk
- 1/2 cup heavy cream
- 1/2 cup grated Parmesan cheese
- 1/4 cup dry white wine (optional)
- 1/2 teaspoon garlic powder
- 1/2 teaspoon onion powder
- 1/4 teaspoon ground nutmeg
- Salt and black pepper, to taste
- 1 cup shredded mozzarella cheese
- Chopped fresh parsley, for garnish

Instructions:

1. Preheat your oven to 350°F (175°C). Grease a 9x13 inch baking dish and set aside.
2. Cook the pasta according to the package instructions until al dente. Drain and set aside.
3. In a large skillet, melt the butter over medium heat. Add the sliced mushrooms and cook until they release their moisture and become golden brown, about 5-7 minutes.
4. Sprinkle the flour over the mushrooms and butter, stirring constantly to cook the flour for about 1-2 minutes, making a roux.
5. Slowly whisk in the chicken broth, milk, and heavy cream, ensuring there are no lumps. Cook, stirring constantly, until the mixture thickens, about 5-7 minutes.
6. Stir in the grated Parmesan cheese, dry white wine (if using), garlic powder, onion powder, nutmeg, salt, and black pepper. Taste and adjust seasoning as needed.
7. Add the cooked diced chicken and cooked pasta to the sauce, stirring until everything is evenly coated.
8. Transfer the chicken and pasta mixture to the prepared baking dish, spreading it out evenly.
9. Sprinkle the shredded mozzarella cheese over the top of the casserole.
10. Bake in the preheated oven for 25-30 minutes, or until the cheese is melted and bubbly and the casserole is heated through.
11. Once done, remove from the oven and let it cool for a few minutes before serving.
12. Garnish with chopped fresh parsley before serving.

Enjoy your Chicken Tetrazzini hot, straight from the oven! It's a comforting and delicious meal that's perfect for feeding a crowd or enjoying as leftovers.

Pork Tenderloin with Apple Compote

Ingredients:

- 1 pork tenderloin (about 1 to 1.5 pounds / 450 to 680g)
- Salt and pepper, to taste
- 2 tablespoons olive oil
- 2 cloves garlic, minced
- 1 teaspoon dried thyme or 1 tablespoon fresh thyme leaves
- 1 teaspoon dried rosemary or 1 tablespoon fresh rosemary leaves, chopped

Instructions:

1. Preheat your oven to 400°F (200°C).

2. Season the pork tenderloin generously with salt and pepper on all sides.
3. In a large oven-safe skillet, heat the olive oil over medium-high heat.
4. Sear the pork tenderloin on all sides until browned, about 2-3 minutes per side.
5. Add the minced garlic, dried thyme, and dried rosemary to the skillet. Stir and cook for about 1 minute until fragrant.
6. Transfer the skillet to the preheated oven and roast the pork tenderloin for about 15-20 minutes, or until it reaches an internal temperature of 145°F (63°C) for medium-rare or 160°F (71°C) for medium, using a meat thermometer inserted into the thickest part of the tenderloin.
7. Once done, remove the skillet from the oven and let the pork rest for 5-10 minutes before slicing.

Apple Compote:

Ingredients:

- 2 large apples, peeled, cored, and diced (such as Granny Smith or Honeycrisp)
- 2 tablespoons unsalted butter
- 2 tablespoons brown sugar
- 1/2 teaspoon ground cinnamon
- Pinch of salt
- 1/4 cup (60ml) apple cider or apple juice

Instructions:

1. In a saucepan, melt the butter over medium heat.
2. Add the diced apples to the saucepan and cook for about 5 minutes, stirring occasionally, until they start to soften.
3. Stir in the brown sugar, ground cinnamon, and a pinch of salt. Cook for another 3-5 minutes until the sugar has dissolved and the apples are tender.
4. Pour in the apple cider or apple juice and simmer for an additional 5 minutes, stirring occasionally, until the liquid has reduced slightly and the compote has thickened.
5. Remove the saucepan from the heat and let the apple compote cool slightly.

Assembly:

Slice the pork tenderloin into medallions and serve with the warm apple compote spooned over the top. Optionally, garnish with fresh thyme or rosemary leaves for extra flavor and presentation.

Enjoy your pork tenderloin with apple compote! It's a perfect dish for a cozy dinner, combining savory and sweet flavors beautifully.

Buffalo Chicken Wraps

Ingredients:

- 2 cups shredded cooked chicken (you can use rotisserie chicken or cook chicken breasts and shred them)
- 1/2 cup buffalo sauce (adjust to taste, depending on how spicy you like it)
- 1/4 cup ranch or blue cheese dressing
- 4 large flour tortillas (you can use whole wheat or gluten-free tortillas if preferred)
- 1 cup shredded lettuce
- 1/2 cup diced tomatoes
- 1/4 cup diced red onion
- 1/2 cup shredded cheddar cheese or crumbled blue cheese (optional)
- Fresh cilantro or parsley, chopped (for garnish, optional)

Instructions:

1. In a mixing bowl, combine the shredded cooked chicken with the buffalo sauce until the chicken is evenly coated.
2. In a separate small bowl, mix together the ranch or blue cheese dressing with a bit of additional buffalo sauce if desired, to taste.
3. Lay out the flour tortillas on a clean surface.
4. Spread a layer of the buffalo chicken mixture onto each tortilla, leaving a border around the edges.
5. Drizzle the ranch or blue cheese dressing over the buffalo chicken mixture on each tortilla.
6. Sprinkle shredded lettuce, diced tomatoes, diced red onion, and shredded cheddar cheese or crumbled blue cheese (if using) evenly over the buffalo chicken mixture on each tortilla.
7. Optional: sprinkle chopped fresh cilantro or parsley over the toppings for added flavor and freshness.
8. Fold in the sides of each tortilla, then roll it up tightly to form a wrap.
9. Repeat with the remaining tortillas and ingredients to make additional wraps.
10. Slice each wrap in half diagonally before serving, if desired.
11. Serve the buffalo chicken wraps immediately, with additional buffalo sauce or dressing on the side for dipping, if desired.

Enjoy your homemade buffalo chicken wraps! They're flavorful, filling, and perfect for serving at parties or enjoying as a quick meal.

Mushroom Risotto

Ingredients:

- 1 1/2 cups Arborio rice
- 4 cups chicken or vegetable broth (warm)
- 1 cup dry white wine
- 2 tablespoons olive oil
- 2 tablespoons butter
- 1 onion, finely chopped
- 2 cloves garlic, minced
- 8 ounces (about 225g) mushrooms (such as cremini, button, or shiitake), sliced
- 1/2 cup grated Parmesan cheese
- Salt and black pepper, to taste
- Fresh parsley, chopped (for garnish)

Instructions:

1. In a saucepan, heat the chicken or vegetable broth over medium heat until warm. Keep it warm on the stove while you prepare the risotto.
2. In a large skillet or wide pot, heat the olive oil and butter over medium heat.
3. Add the finely chopped onion to the skillet and cook until translucent, about 5 minutes.
4. Add the minced garlic to the skillet and cook for another minute until fragrant.
5. Add the sliced mushrooms to the skillet and cook until they release their moisture and become golden brown, about 5-7 minutes.
6. Add the Arborio rice to the skillet and stir to coat the rice with the oil and butter, toasting it slightly, about 2 minutes.
7. Pour in the dry white wine and stir constantly until the wine is absorbed by the rice.
8. Begin adding the warm broth to the skillet, one ladleful at a time, stirring frequently and allowing each addition to be absorbed by the rice before adding more. This process will take about 18-20 minutes. The risotto should be creamy and the rice should be tender but still slightly firm (al dente).
9. Once the risotto is cooked to your desired consistency, stir in the grated Parmesan cheese until melted and creamy. Season with salt and black pepper to taste.
10. Remove the skillet from the heat and let the risotto rest for a minute or two before serving.
11. Serve the mushroom risotto hot, garnished with chopped fresh parsley.

Enjoy your homemade mushroom risotto! It's a comforting and flavorful dish that's perfect for a cozy dinner.

Cajun Jambalaya

Ingredients:

- 1 pound (about 450g) chicken breasts or thighs, cut into bite-sized pieces
- 1/2 pound (about 225g) smoked sausage or andouille sausage, sliced
- 1 tablespoon Cajun seasoning (store-bought or homemade)
- 2 tablespoons olive oil
- 1 onion, chopped
- 1 bell pepper, chopped
- 2 stalks celery, chopped
- 3 cloves garlic, minced
- 1 can (14 oz or 400g) diced tomatoes
- 3 cups chicken broth
- 1 1/2 cups long-grain white rice
- Salt and black pepper, to taste
- Chopped green onions, for garnish
- Chopped fresh parsley, for garnish

Instructions:

1. In a large bowl, season the chicken pieces with Cajun seasoning, making sure they are evenly coated.
2. In a large skillet or Dutch oven, heat the olive oil over medium-high heat.
3. Add the seasoned chicken pieces to the skillet and cook until browned on all sides, about 5-7 minutes. Remove the chicken from the skillet and set aside.
4. In the same skillet, add the sliced sausage and cook until browned, about 5 minutes. Remove the sausage from the skillet and set aside.
5. Add the chopped onion, bell pepper, and celery to the skillet. Cook, stirring occasionally, until the vegetables are softened, about 5 minutes.
6. Stir in the minced garlic and cook for another minute until fragrant.
7. Add the diced tomatoes (with their juices) to the skillet, scraping up any browned bits from the bottom of the skillet.
8. Return the cooked chicken and sausage to the skillet.
9. Pour in the chicken broth and bring the mixture to a boil.
10. Stir in the rice, then reduce the heat to low, cover, and simmer for about 20-25 minutes, or until the rice is cooked and most of the liquid is absorbed.

11. Once the rice is cooked, season the jambalaya with salt and black pepper to taste.
12. Remove the skillet from the heat and let the jambalaya rest for a few minutes before serving.
13. Garnish the jambalaya with chopped green onions and fresh parsley before serving.

Enjoy your homemade Cajun jambalaya! It's a flavorful and comforting dish that's perfect for feeding a crowd or enjoying as leftovers.

Swedish Meatballs

Ingredients:

For the meatballs:

- 1 pound (about 450g) ground beef (or a mixture of beef and pork)
- 1/2 cup breadcrumbs
- 1/4 cup milk
- 1 small onion, finely chopped or grated
- 1 garlic clove, minced
- 1 egg
- 1/2 teaspoon salt
- 1/4 teaspoon black pepper
- 1/4 teaspoon ground nutmeg
- 1/4 teaspoon ground allspice

For the sauce:

- 2 tablespoons unsalted butter
- 2 tablespoons all-purpose flour
- 2 cups beef broth
- 1/2 cup heavy cream
- 1 tablespoon soy sauce
- Salt and black pepper, to taste
- Chopped fresh parsley, for garnish

Instructions:

1. In a large mixing bowl, combine the breadcrumbs and milk. Let it sit for a few minutes until the breadcrumbs have absorbed the milk.
2. Add the ground beef, chopped onion, minced garlic, egg, salt, black pepper, nutmeg, and allspice to the bowl with the soaked breadcrumbs. Mix until well combined.
3. Shape the meat mixture into small meatballs, about 1 inch in diameter.
4. In a large skillet, heat 1 tablespoon of butter over medium heat. Add the meatballs in batches and cook until browned on all sides and cooked through, about 8-10 minutes. Remove the meatballs from the skillet and set aside.
5. In the same skillet, melt the remaining 1 tablespoon of butter over medium heat. Sprinkle the flour over the melted butter and cook, stirring constantly, for about 1 minute to make a roux.
6. Slowly pour in the beef broth, whisking constantly to prevent lumps from forming.
7. Stir in the heavy cream and soy sauce. Continue to cook, stirring occasionally, until the sauce thickens, about 5-7 minutes.
8. Season the sauce with salt and black pepper to taste.
9. Return the cooked meatballs to the skillet, tossing gently to coat them in the sauce. Let them simmer in the sauce for a few minutes to heat through.
10. Garnish the Swedish meatballs with chopped fresh parsley before serving.
11. Serve the Swedish meatballs hot, either as an appetizer or as a main dish, over cooked egg noodles or mashed potatoes.

Enjoy your homemade Swedish meatballs! They're a comforting and delicious meal that's perfect for any occasion.

Ratatouille Stuffed Peppers

Ingredients:

- 4 large bell peppers (any color), halved and seeds removed
- 2 tablespoons olive oil
- 1 onion, diced
- 2 cloves garlic, minced
- 1 eggplant, diced
- 2 zucchini, diced
- 1 yellow squash, diced
- 1 red bell pepper, diced
- 1 can (14 oz or 400g) diced tomatoes
- 1 teaspoon dried thyme
- 1 teaspoon dried oregano
- Salt and black pepper, to taste
- 1/2 cup grated Parmesan cheese

- Fresh basil leaves, chopped (for garnish)

Instructions:

1. Preheat your oven to 375°F (190°C).
2. Heat olive oil in a large skillet over medium heat. Add the diced onion and garlic and sauté until softened, about 3-4 minutes.
3. Add the diced eggplant, zucchini, yellow squash, and red bell pepper to the skillet. Cook, stirring occasionally, until the vegetables are tender, about 8-10 minutes.
4. Stir in the diced tomatoes, dried thyme, dried oregano, salt, and black pepper. Cook for another 5 minutes, allowing the flavors to meld together.
5. While the ratatouille mixture is cooking, prepare the bell peppers. Cut each bell pepper in half lengthwise and remove the seeds and membranes.
6. Place the bell pepper halves in a baking dish, cut side up.
7. Spoon the ratatouille mixture evenly into each bell pepper half, pressing down gently to pack the filling.
8. Sprinkle grated Parmesan cheese over the top of each stuffed pepper.
9. Cover the baking dish with foil and bake in the preheated oven for 25-30 minutes, or until the peppers are tender and the filling is heated through.
10. Remove the foil and bake for an additional 5-10 minutes, or until the cheese is melted and golden brown.
11. Once done, remove the stuffed peppers from the oven and let them cool slightly.
12. Garnish with chopped fresh basil leaves before serving.

Enjoy your ratatouille stuffed peppers! They're a delicious and nutritious vegetarian meal that's perfect for any occasion.

Korean Beef Bowls

Ingredients:

For the beef:

- 1 pound (about 450g) thinly sliced beef (such as sirloin or ribeye)
- 1/4 cup soy sauce
- 2 tablespoons brown sugar
- 2 tablespoons sesame oil
- 2 cloves garlic, minced
- 1 teaspoon grated ginger

- 2 green onions, chopped (white and green parts separated)
- 1 tablespoon toasted sesame seeds
- 1 tablespoon vegetable oil, for cooking

For serving:

- Cooked rice (white or brown)
- Thinly sliced cucumber
- Shredded carrots
- Sliced avocado
- Kimchi (optional)
- Sesame seeds, for garnish
- Sriracha or gochujang (Korean chili paste), for extra heat (optional)

Instructions:

1. In a bowl, combine the soy sauce, brown sugar, sesame oil, minced garlic, grated ginger, chopped white parts of green onions, and toasted sesame seeds. Stir until the sugar is dissolved and the marinade is well mixed.
2. Add the thinly sliced beef to the marinade and toss until the beef is evenly coated. Cover the bowl and marinate in the refrigerator for at least 30 minutes, or up to 4 hours for maximum flavor.
3. Heat vegetable oil in a large skillet or wok over medium-high heat.
4. Add the marinated beef to the skillet, spreading it out into an even layer. Cook for 2-3 minutes without stirring to allow the beef to caramelize and develop a nice sear.
5. Stir-fry the beef for an additional 2-3 minutes, or until cooked through and no longer pink.
6. Remove the skillet from the heat and sprinkle the chopped green parts of the green onions over the cooked beef. Toss to combine.
7. To serve, divide the cooked rice among serving bowls. Top each bowl with a portion of the cooked beef.
8. Arrange the sliced cucumber, shredded carrots, and sliced avocado on top of the beef.
9. Garnish the Korean beef bowls with additional sesame seeds and a drizzle of sriracha or gochujang for extra heat, if desired.
10. Serve immediately and enjoy your homemade Korean beef bowls!

These Korean beef bowls are customizable, so feel free to add or substitute your favorite vegetables or toppings to suit your taste preferences.

Creamy Pesto Chicken Pasta

Ingredients:

- 8 ounces (about 225g) pasta (such as spaghetti, fettuccine, or penne)
- 2 boneless, skinless chicken breasts, cut into bite-sized pieces
- Salt and black pepper, to taste
- 2 tablespoons olive oil
- 2 cloves garlic, minced
- 1/2 cup chicken broth
- 1/2 cup heavy cream
- 1/4 cup basil pesto (store-bought or homemade)
- 1 cup cherry tomatoes, halved
- 1/2 cup grated Parmesan cheese
- Fresh basil leaves, chopped, for garnish (optional)

Instructions:

1. Cook the pasta according to the package instructions until al dente. Drain and set aside.
2. Season the chicken breast pieces with salt and black pepper on both sides.
3. In a large skillet, heat the olive oil over medium-high heat. Add the seasoned chicken pieces to the skillet and cook until browned and cooked through, about 6-8 minutes. Remove the chicken from the skillet and set aside.
4. In the same skillet, add the minced garlic and cook for about 1 minute until fragrant.
5. Pour in the chicken broth and scrape up any browned bits from the bottom of the skillet.
6. Add the heavy cream to the skillet and bring the mixture to a simmer.
7. Stir in the basil pesto until well combined and the sauce is smooth and creamy.
8. Add the cooked pasta, cooked chicken, and halved cherry tomatoes to the skillet. Stir until everything is evenly coated in the creamy pesto sauce.
9. Cook for an additional 2-3 minutes, stirring occasionally, until the pasta is heated through and the sauce has thickened slightly.
10. Remove the skillet from the heat and sprinkle grated Parmesan cheese over the pasta. Toss gently to combine.
11. Garnish with chopped fresh basil leaves, if desired.
12. Serve the creamy pesto chicken pasta hot, with additional Parmesan cheese on the side if desired.

Enjoy your homemade creamy pesto chicken pasta! It's a satisfying and flavorful meal that's perfect for any occasion.

Veggie-Packed Quinoa Salad

Ingredients:

- 1 cup quinoa, rinsed
- 2 cups water or vegetable broth
- 1 cup cherry tomatoes, halved
- 1 cucumber, diced
- 1 bell pepper, diced (any color)
- 1/2 red onion, finely chopped
- 1/2 cup chopped fresh parsley
- 1/4 cup chopped fresh basil
- 1/4 cup crumbled feta cheese (optional)
- 1/4 cup sliced black olives (optional)

For the dressing:

- 1/4 cup extra-virgin olive oil
- 2 tablespoons lemon juice
- 1 clove garlic, minced
- 1 teaspoon Dijon mustard
- 1/2 teaspoon honey or maple syrup (optional)
- Salt and black pepper, to taste

Instructions:

1. In a medium saucepan, combine the quinoa and water or vegetable broth. Bring to a boil over high heat, then reduce the heat to low, cover, and simmer for 15-20 minutes, or until the quinoa is cooked and the liquid is absorbed. Remove from heat and let it cool slightly.
2. In a large bowl, combine the cooked quinoa, cherry tomatoes, cucumber, bell pepper, red onion, chopped parsley, and chopped basil. Toss to combine.
3. If using, add the crumbled feta cheese and sliced black olives to the bowl and gently toss again.
4. In a small bowl, whisk together the extra-virgin olive oil, lemon juice, minced garlic, Dijon mustard, honey or maple syrup (if using), salt, and black pepper until well combined.
5. Pour the dressing over the quinoa salad and toss until everything is evenly coated.
6. Taste and adjust seasoning, adding more salt and black pepper if needed.
7. Chill the quinoa salad in the refrigerator for at least 30 minutes to allow the flavors to meld together.
8. Before serving, give the salad a final toss and garnish with additional fresh herbs, if desired.

9. Serve the veggie-packed quinoa salad chilled or at room temperature as a light and refreshing meal or side dish.

Enjoy your homemade veggie-packed quinoa salad! It's nutritious, flavorful, and packed with wholesome ingredients.

www.ingramcontent.com/pod-product-compliance
Lightning Source LLC
LaVergne TN
LVHW062051070526
838201LV00080B/2314

9798330208494